THE Idaho Table

THE
Idaho
Table

A Taste of the Intermountain West

Jonathan R. Mortimer

Photography by Greg Sims

Holdthebaby Publishing
Boise, Idaho

Although the author and publisher have made every effort to ensure the accuracy and completeness of information contained in this book, we assume no responsibility for errors, inaccuracies, omissions, or any inconsistency herein. Any slights of people, places, or organizations are unintentional.

Photographer: Greg Sims, Sims Studios

First printing 2003

ISBN 0-9724333-2-5
LCCN 2002112870

ATTENTION CORPORATIONS, UNIVERSITIES, COLLEGES, AND PROFESSIONAL ORGANIZATIONS: Quantity discounts are available on bulk purchases of this book for educational, gift purposes, or as premiums for increasing magazine subscriptions or renewals. Special books or book excerpts can also be created to fit specific needs. For information, please contact Holdthebaby Publishing, 1207 E. Lexington Court, Boise, ID 83706; ph. 208-338-6550.

*To my wife, Shara, who makes me
a better person and chef everyday.*

*And to my father, Lee, who always
encouraged my dreams.*

■ *Table of Contents*

Preface

Mortimer's restaurant encompasses what *The Idaho Table* is all about. We serve dinners five nights a week with local and regional product. I have always felt lucky to cook in Idaho's capitol city just a few miles from the farmers' fields and ranchers' rangeland. It is this proximity to the great foods of this region that has inspired these recipes. The techniques are not really all that difficult, but do require discerning procurement of fresh product. (A large backyard garden does not hurt either!) It sounds a lot like the way a good cook does it at home because that is what we are trying to achieve at the restaurant. Meals filled with love and passion with an intimate understanding of every item that goes into a dish. We have fun in our kitchen and that can't help but find its way onto the plate.

My culinary life began when my father moved our family from New York to the resort town of Sun Valley, Idaho. A few years later at the age of fourteen I started my first kitchen job (I may have led them to believe I was sixteen) prepping the salad bar at a busy steakhouse. It was not long before heavy snow fell, everyone went skiing, and subsequently no one showed up to work—no one except me. I was rapidly promoted to broiler chef because of the lack of other options. The truth was that I was small of stature and needed to stand on a milk crate just to reach. The stress was a bit much at times for a person of my age and I soon realized that this business holds no quarter. Young or old, strong or weak, you had to perform…you had to produce. The chef at this restaurant was a throwback. Hippie may be too strong a word, but he had this phrase that became the cornerstone of my culinary career: "Isn't food cool?"

The next fifteen years happened at a dizzying pace. In that time I opened numerous restaurants (sometimes three in a year) for several different companies. At the end I appreciated the experience that I had gained, however, I wanted to get back to Idaho, to feel like I was home again. After brief stints at several upscale Boise eateries my wife Shara and I bought our first restaurant, B.B. Strand's. An attorney and land developer had built it in an eighty-year-old building that had been many things to many people. He was a tough businessman but a kind person. We became good friends through the process and to this day he is truly one of my heroes. We did well and as much as I thought I knew about the restaurant business, owning our own place was like getting a restaurant master's degree. It was here that I was able to cultivate my own style of cooking, not being burdened by corporate specifications or regional managers.

One of the most important things that happened during these years was that I made relationships with farmers, ranchers, mushroom foragers, and fisherman. I went to the orchards to pick my own apples and trimmed the grapevines in the vineyards above the Snake River. I learned about this great oasis in the desert that was made possible by incredibly hard work and irrigation. I learned to truly understand the tastes and aromas. I learned how to create meals that are as subtle to the palate as rain on the desert sage is to the nose. I am an avid bicyclist and on my long rides I would just intoxicate my senses with the sights, sounds, and smells of the farms.

Mortimer's is the culmination of everything learned before gaining the confidence of knowing that we only have to artistically fulfill ourselves. It took a little doing but we acquired a team that could make it happen. That could decipher the dream from the night before and make it happen today. The parts whose sum proves to be much greater than we could have ever imagined. The people who could, over time, create an institution as opposed to just another restaurant.

This restaurant has restored my culinary faith. Once again I see no life for me except that as a chef. The recipes in this book have come along all this way, ever changing until they are either completely different from where they started or, at times, right back where they started. The only underlying theme is Idaho and the Northwest. You won't have to search hither and yon for the ingredients to create these recipes. They are right in our own backyard beckoning for you to bring them to *The Idaho Table*.

Tools for Idaho Cuisine

Pots and pans

Much of what we are going to do in this book requires the use of pots and pans. The quality of these tools is extremely important and when purchasing these items a few things need to be kept in mind. For sauce work generally nonreactive pans made from either stainless steel or copper are best. They need to have a thicker than normal bottom that distributes heat evenly and provides a buffer from burning. For sauté pans the same ideas generally apply. One thing you must have is a high quality, nonstick sauté pan. Make sure when using your nonstick pan that you don't use metal spatulas or utensils with them since they scratch the finish. Also, you want to avoid extremely high heat, since that also weakens the finish. The last essential pot is a high quality stockpot with at least a two-gallon capacity. Many of the recipes in this book require cooking with stock to boost the layers of flavor that create a truly unique dish. Stocks give you the true essence of flavor and need to be made and processed with great care.

Knives

I don't believe there is a recipe in this book that can be made without the use of a knife. With this in mind, it is essential you have high quality, extremely sharp knives for your work. The three styles of knives you can't live without are:

1. A chef's knife at least eight and preferably ten inches long

2. A boning knife with some flexibility to the blade

3. A serrated knife at least ten inches in length

There are a lot of world-class knives available and many have there own unique attributes. The key to purchasing your knives should be how they feel in your hand. Only by holding a knife can you test a true comfort level with it; that along with the quality of the steel are the only two factors that should be considered when buying knives.

The grill

We do a lot of grilling at the restaurant; however, we seldom complete the entire cooking process on the grill. To me the grill has two uses: to season and to sear. As you will see in many of the recipes in the book, items are placed on a grill for short periods of time only to impart flavor and sear or seal the natural juices in the item that you are cooking. Then the item is often transferred to the oven where the more even heat can do a better job of finishing the cooking.

Gas grills are great for convenience. However, they lack the soul, character, and especially the flavor a real wood-fired grill can impart. My favorite in the years gone by is the applewood-fired grill we had at B.B. Strand's. The rich flavor of this grill from the intensely perfumed smoke that came from the local orchards I have yet to duplicate. If you want the convenience of a gas grill and the aroma of smoke, you can use the following technique. Soak four to five chunks of hardwood in water for 20 minutes then strain off the water. Heat the gas grill in your usual manner, but just prior to placing the items on the grill lift the grill up with a pair of tongs and place the soaked hardwood chunks on the lava stones. Let the grill back down and place the items on the grill, cooking them as the recipe indicates. It is a good idea to keep a spray bottle of water on hand to put out flare-ups because the hot wood wants to catch fire. Keep the lid on the grill as much as possible to trap the aromatic smoke around the meat.

As for the grill itself, you should brush it with a wire brush and oil it with an oil rag before and after use. Avoid washing a grill with soap, since that removes the natural seasoning from the grill and cause meats and especially fish to stick.

Smokers

A lot of the same effects achieved with the above-mentioned grill technique could be achieved with a smoker, but to a much more intense level. Smoking was a favored way for the Indians along the Snake River to preserve their catch of trout, bass, and birds to reserve for the winter months. A lot of people are intimidated by smoking, but it is not nearly as complicated a process as it may appear.

Home smokers are available at many retail outlets and mail order sources. It is important that the smoker you buy has the ability to control the temperature. Also look for a "fire box" that is contained and independent from the smoking chamber.

As with the grilling process, soak the manufacturers recommended amount of hardwood chunks in water for 20 minutes or so prior to putting them in the smoker. Place them in the firebox and turn the thermostat to the recipe-specified temperature. I often coat the racks of my smoker with olive oil to minimize sticking during smoking especially when smoking fish. Often you can adjust the amount of smoke flavor imparted by opening and closing vents on the top and the sides of the unit; however, I recommend you not close these vents completely since the smoke can settle inside and cause a bitter taste.

Blenders and immersion blenders

Much of the sauces and soups in this book require pureeing and there are several valuable pieces of equipment you can use. My favorite piece of "plug in" equipment is my immersion blender. This is a handheld blender with a small blade at the bottom of a shaft that operates at a very fast rpm. An immersion blender can be placed right into your soup or saucepan and rapidly processes large quantities of soup or sauce to an incredibly smooth texture. The real advantage over traditional blenders or food processors is that you don't have to transfer an often very hot liquid to process it; it can be done right in its existing pan while you continue to cook it. Immersion blenders can be purchased for as little as fifty dollars; however, you always seem to get what you pay for. A commercial grade immersion blender can cost as much as nine hundred dollars, but this is a piece of equipment that can process as much as 5 gallons at a time and would surely be overkill for home use.

A quality food processor or blender can achieve the same goal as an immersion blender; it is just slightly more inconvenient to both use and clean. As with any other piece of equipment you need to buy a quality unit paying special attention the strength of the motor. With food processors it is a good idea to get one with a "pulse" mode since it is useful when you need to coarse chop things like nuts or onions. When purchasing blenders make sure to get one with a reasonable amount of capacity. Many blenders for sale only handle a quart or less of liquid without running over the top when turned on.

■ *Techniques for Idaho Cuisine*

Roasting garlic

Every recipe in this book that calls for garlic uses roasted garlic. Roasted garlic has a much softer and sweeter flavor than its raw counterpart. To roast garlic, preheat an oven to 300 degrees. Cut the top ¼ inch off the bulbs of garlic and place them in a roasting pan with sides slightly taller than the garlic bulbs. Pour 1 tablespoon of olive oil over each clove of garlic and season them with salt and fresh ground pepper. Cover the pan with an oven-safe lid or foil and place them in the oven for 1 hour and 15 minutes. Upon inspection of the garlic, the flesh should have turned golden brown and started to jump out of the husks. The sweet garlic inside should be a jelly-like substance that easily squeezes out of the husks.

Puree the roasted garlic in a blender or food processor with enough olive oil to make a smooth puree. This is the finished roasted garlic that the recipes call for. The other luxury this affords is that it can be added to a recipe at virtually any point so that it doesn't have to risk being burned.

Roasting peppers and chilies

Roasting peppers and chilies, much like roasting garlic, unleashes the true sweet flavor while eliminating the bitter and acidic flavors. Generally I roast my peppers and chilies over the grill, but they can also be done in a very hot oven, or over a burner by holding them with a fork. To prepare the pepper or chili I wash it then dry it with a towel. Lightly coat the exterior with olive oil and place over high heat on a grill. I cook each side for about 2 minutes or until it is completely blackened. Once it is charred on all sides place the peppers or chilies in a bowl and cover with a lid for about 20 minutes. This allows them to "sweat" and makes removing the skin much easier.

At this point the blackened skin should be easy to remove by simply peeling with your fingers or rubbing with a towel. Once the charred skin is removed, pop the stem out and rinse the remaining flesh with cold water to remove any seeds and fragments of charred skin. The flesh of the roasted chili is now ready to use.

Preparing shallots

We use a lot of shallots at the restaurant. The subtle and sweet taste of shallots is impossible to duplicate. I've heard many say that shallots are a flavor cross between onions and garlic, but to me they have a distinct flavor all their own.

When selecting shallots at the market be sure to stick with relatively small ones since they have a sweeter and less acidic flavor than their larger counterpart. As with so many things in America, we have used our technological advances to grow shallots large, and in so doing we have robbed them of their precious delicate flavor along the way.

Because of the amount of shallots we use in the restaurant, we preserve them in white wine after peeling and fine chopping them. This step is not necessary if you are simply peeling and chopping enough for a single recipe. But if you find yourself using shallots frequently, you can keep them in the refrigerator for several days by covering them with white wine.

Preparing breadcrumbs

There are a number of recipes in this book that require coating items with breadcrumbs or a breadcrumb mixture with nuts, herbs, or seeds. A high-quality breadcrumb is essential for a crisp and tasty breading.

At the restaurant we have the advantage of baking our own unique breads and taking the leftovers and making breadcrumbs out of them. Because we have many different flavors of breads, I try to match up flavor profiles of the bread with the dish I'm working with.

We prepare the bread by cutting it into slices, laying it out on a baking sheet, and placing it in a 250-degree oven for 45 minutes or so until it is dry, but not overly browned. At this point we either use a cheese grater for coarse crumbs or we place it in a food processor for fine crumbs. While this is certainly more work than buying premade crumbs at the store, it is well worth the effort. Remember when selecting bread for this purpose, the better the quality of the bread, the better the crumb.

Washing fruits and vegetables

It is often hard to tell at a glance just how clean a piece of fruit or vegetable is. Bacteria, some hazardous and some not, are on everything we eat, and we need bacteria to survive. Harmful bacteria, however, cannot simply be rinsed off in cold water, although many pesticide and chemical residues can. There are some new products on the market, mostly made from vegetable-derived alcohols that advertise significant reduction of bacterial growth on foods washed with these products. I have recently seen several independent studies that disprove this, however, so it seems the decision lies with the consumer.

When I take tomatoes fresh from the garden, I like to enjoy them au naturel. Even a brisk rinse in cold water seems to take away the taste of the sun these gems possess. Most commercially grown produce undergoes a number of washing procedures along the way to ensure a safe product hits the market. The bottom line is that if you know your source you can decide what method is best to present a safe fruit or vegetable.

At the restaurant we generally wash all produce in cold water to eliminate soil, sand, and occasionally bugs (especially on organic produce). The best way we have found to do this is by filling a meticulously cleaned sink with cold water and allowing the unwanted particles to sink to the bottom. The most important part of this is to remove the vegetables from the sink prior to draining it. If you drain the sink with the vegetables still in it, the produce comes back in contact with the unwanted particles that have been liberated and then come to rest on the bottom of the sink.

The one thing I seldom wash is mushrooms. We love mushrooms for their earthy and natural flavor and I have always found those flavors dissipate when they are scrubbed. I seldom use commercially grown mushrooms at the restaurant and I always inspect them thoroughly for parasites and the ever-present pine needle that comes with them. For button mushrooms grown in commercial medium, I am much more apt to give them a good scrub with a mushroom brush.

Ultimately the washing of produce comes down to you and your peace of mind. Obviously when items are to be cooked the safety factor is greatly improved. The single best thing you can do, however, is to know your source and stay away from anything that does not have a healthy appearance.

Blanching vegetables

There are a number of reasons blanching vegetables is necessary. The main reason for blanching is much like searing meats: It shocks them into locking their flavors inside. With vegetables there is also the added bonus of bringing out their brilliant colors. Often if I am incorporating several different types of vegetables in a dish, I blanch the ones that take longer so when I add all the vegetables to the dish the cooking times are congruent.

The blanching of vegetables is a simple yet exact science. Start by bringing to a boil enough water to completely submerge the vegetables, and add enough kosher or sea salt to make the water mildly yet decidedly salty. Have a bowl of ice water ready then add the vegetables to the pot. Allow the vegetables to cook until they are bright in color but not at all soft. Strain the vegetables from the water and place them in the ice water until they are completely cooled. Strain the water off the vegetables yet again and they are now blanched and ready to add to your recipe.

Roasting nuts and seeds

Every recipe in this book that contains either nuts or seeds requires roasting. Roasting brings the oils contained inside to the flavor forefront and lends a considerably greater impact to the dish.

The roasting process is simple. Place the nuts or seeds in a nonstick sauté pan and put them in a 400-degree oven for about 10 minutes. Remove the pan from the oven, toss the nuts or seeds, then place the pan back in the oven. Continue this process several times until golden brown and extremely fragrant. When done, take the nuts or seeds out of the pan and place them in a dish to cool. After cooling they can be chopped or added to the recipe as required.

Preparing fresh herbs

I am a huge fan of fresh herbs and choose fresh over dried almost any day. Fresh herbs always have a much more subtle and honest flavor. Ten years ago this was a problem for the chef at home, but this has changed dramatically in the past several years. Virtually any market carries basil, dill, tarragon, rosemary, and thyme these days, and often they are of great quality.

When I use fresh herbs as an addition to a dish, I remove the leaf from the stem. (I often use the stems to impart flavors to stocks.) I chop the leaves to the specifications of the recipe. Some leaves, such as thyme or tarragon, are delicate and subtle enough to use as a whole leaf and give a dish a nice visual appearance.

When selecting fresh herbs look for a bright green color with no traces of decomposition. They should smell fresh and not have a grassy or dried-hay aroma. One simple way to have great herbs year-round is a window herb garden. As with all fresh produce, an herb picked at the time of use lends subtler flavor than one that has spent a week at the vegetable market.

Preparing spices

When buying spices it is always better to remember that whole spice is better; for instance, a cinnamon stick is better than ground cinnamon. The reason for this is the simple process of oxidation, which robs flavors and oils from spices. The less surface area there is, the less oxidation can occur.

There are several tools that are needed to render spices to a usable form for your recipe. One is a spice grater. A spice grater looks like a very fine cheese grater that is often slightly curved. Graters work well for softer spices like nutmeg. For more brittle spices and seeds used for seasoning, a coffee mill works well. Often I toast the spice (see *Roasting nuts and seeds*) then process them to their usable form by using a coffee mill I use only for spices. After pulsing the item in the mill to its desired state, simply wipe out the mill with a dry towel and it is ready for the next use. Try to render only enough spice for the recipe you are working with, since saving rendered spices puts you back into the oxidation cycle.

Caring for potatoes

One of the greatest things about potatoes is that they have a long shelf life. This, however, should not be taken for granted. As with all produce, a potato that is fresh from the ground has a silkier texture and more potato flavor than one that has been stored for six months. Although fresh potatoes are not always available, several things must be kept in mind for proper storage. Potatoes need to be stored in a cool, dry place with proper ventilation. At the restaurant we find that milk crates make a great storage bin for potatoes. They allow good airflow and resist the harboring of mold and bacterial growth. We stack the crates in a cool dry closet and can keep them in great shape for several months.

Another thing to remember is that different varieties of potatoes store better than others. I have found that I can keep russets in great condition for several months, but reds start to get soft and have black heart after several weeks. Finding what potatoes store right for you takes a bit of experimentation, but I always like to have several different varieties of potatoes on hand since they are either an ingredient or accompaniment to many of my recipes.

Marinating

A number of the meat recipes in this book require marinating. Marinating imparts subtle flavors to meat that can't be achieved by simply sprinkling on herbs and spices. The other quality the marinating can impart is tenderizing. Marinating, however, can have a reverse effect if simple guidelines are not followed. It is important to remember that the tenderizing effects of marinades generally reach full effect in several hours. After that the meat actually takes on so much moisture it becomes tougher.

For more tender cuts of meat I want to impart flavor to, I use a vacuum marinater. These units can be as simple as a hand pump and as sophisticated as an electric pump, but they all work the same way. When the atmospheric pressure is removed from the vessel, the pores of the meat open and allow the marinade to flow freely inside. The beauty of this is that it can achieve better results in 10 minutes than several hours of traditional marinating.

▩ *Guide to Necessary Foods*

Bacon

There are several producers of great bacon in Idaho. Because bacon is generally used as a flavor ingredient in the recipes in this book, you need to buy a quality product. My choice for flavor reasons alone is applewood-smoked bacon. It has an incredibly aromatic flavor that is not overpowering. Look for a ratio of meat equal to that of the fat. Remember, bacon is quite salty, so you need to be careful when adding salt to a dish with bacon in it.

Barley

Barley's greatest use is in the beer-making process. I have found that it has a great texture and does a good job of taking on the subtle flavors of items with which it is being cooked. When selecting barley I always lean toward product from the panhandle of Idaho. The same rich soil that produces such great wheat does well by barley also. Look for plump berries of barley with little "dust" at the bottom of the bag (a sign that it has been damaged during processing and shipping).

Beans (fresh)

Haricot verts: This is a strain of French bean. Many people refer to them as "baby" beans, because full grown they tend to be smaller than their counterparts. Haricot verts have great eye appeal and a sweet flavor. To be enjoyed, they don't need much more than to be quickly blanched in salted water, strained, and tossed with butter.

Wax beans: Similar to haricot verts but yellow in color, I often see these beans overgrown and too large in markets, which gives them a pasty texture. Look for beans that are around 3 inches long and not much more than ¼ inch around. They have a slightly more citrus-like flavor than green beans and great eye appeal on a plate.

Green beans: A kin of blue lake beans and often just called local beans in the markets, these beans have a vibrant color and can be as long as 5 inches in length. The season for these beans in some years can be as long as five months ranging from late June to early November. They can either be enjoyed whole or cut in 1-inch sections and added to a stew or casserole at the last minute, lending both farm fresh flavor and eye appeal.

European flat beans: These are not readily available in markets because they can't be harvested with mechanical harvesters. They can be as long as 10 inches and as wide as 1 inch. We get them through local organic gardeners at the restaurant and are a worthy addition to your backyard garden. They are so unique-looking that we just blanch them leaving them crisp, toss in butter, and serve them with steaks for a stunning visual presentation, since they curl all over the plate.

Beans (dried)

White northern beans are the most readily available dried beans harvested in the state. These have a sweet flavor and great texture that adds to any soup or stew. If you want to infuse these beans with flavor they can be boiled in stock instead of water. They should be fully cooked before adding to a dish.

Kidney beans are also grown in Idaho with some success. These beans make a great refried bean for Mexican-inspired dishes and are also a fine addition to soups and stews.

Black beans are also available in virtually any market in Idaho. I like to soak these beans overnight and then cook them al dente. After rinsing thoroughly, they can be added to your favorite salsa recipe to add a great color contrast as well as texture.

Bell pepper

Whether red, yellow, or green (the same pepper at different stages of growth), bell peppers add both a sweet flavor and great color to any dish. Generally, I roast bell peppers to intensify their sweet flavor and remove the somewhat bitter outer skin.

Butter

While there is nothing unique to Idaho about butter there is always "better" butter available in any market. Generally the higher the butterfat content the higher the price. After spending time in Europe I realized that most great restaurants make their own butter, and the flavor and texture difference is substantial. In the past few years there have been products hitting the markets billed as "gourmet" or "European" butter. Although these products are more expensive, they often have a creamier texture and more butter flavor. Another thing to keep in mind with butter is that if the recipe calls for unsalted butter, make sure to use just that. It is amazing how much salt there is in regular butter and not using unsalted butter can make your recipe too salty.

Catfish

Catfish has a long history in Idaho. For some of the Indian tribes the catfish that lived in the pools of some of the slower moving rivers and lakes was a staple of their diet. In modern times we have cultivated them, and they have become prolific through the advent of aquaculture. I think many people pass up catfish because of their ugly outward appearance. The filets that lie inside, however, are as beautiful and flavorful as any fish that abounds in our state.

Cheeses

Goats milk cheese is starting to gain its share of small producers in the state. The most abundantly available is *fromage blanc,* a creamy white cheese with a mildly piquant flavor. The uses of this cheese are many, but I find it is best enjoyed with a somewhat acidic accompanying flavor to cut the sometimes overpowering richness of the cheese.

Cheddar is a favorite cheese in Idaho as it is in the rest of America. It has an incredibly approachable and understandable flavor. The best cheddars are an unadulterated white color or very mildly yellow, not the bright orange that is popular. Without the food dyes you'll not only find a much sharper flavor, but a more crumbly and honest texture. You'll also find it does not melt as evenly and readily without the additives, but this is a small tradeoff for the true flavor.

Mozzarella is always a favorite of ours at the restaurant and we use it for everything from stuffing polenta to holding together vegetable gratins. In Idaho there are a few companies that make "fresh" mozzarella that requires being held in brine to maintain its freshness until use. This cheese can be challenging to use because it melts so quickly. While it does cook well if you are quick, its delicate flavor and texture may be best suited to enjoying chilled with tomato slices, fresh basil, and balsamic vinegar. However you choose to enjoy this dairy treasure do not pass it up because of its different storage situation. A quick rinse of the brine and you are ready to enjoy one of your finest cheese experiences ever.

Bleu cheese is produced throughout the Northwest, and there are several large producers of this full-flavored cheese in Idaho. I always try to be true to my immediate surroundings; however, I find the varieties of Oregon cave aged bleu to be my favorite. Many modern practices "rush" the aging/molding process through chemical and controlled atmospheric means and this gives the cheese a "chemical burn," as we call it in our kitchen. There are several different makers on the Oregon coast that age the cheese naturally. This drives up the price, but there is no comparison to its high quality.

Parmesan is made throughout the country and with the quality of what is available in the United States there is really no reason to go to the trouble of importing it from Europe. The key to working with Parmesan is to leave the block or wheel intact with the rind on until needed, at which point you should grind only what you need. Like herbs and spices there is a great flavor loss through oxidation, and the more surface area you expose to the atmosphere the more rapid the flavor loss. People are often confused as to the difference between Parmesan and Romano. The difference is only aging time. For Parmesan to become Romano, the cheese must be aged for ninety days. This aging time produces a stronger, nuttier flavor.

Chicken

Free-range chickens have some advantages and disadvantages. They are often more full flavored but can be a bit tough. In recent years there has been a concern that they could be more susceptible to be a carrier of salmonella because of the way they are raised. If you can find a good and reputable producer of free-range chickens, don't miss out on this more flavorful alternative to the mainstream. Be prepared to pay about a dollar more per pound for this pleasure.

"Natural" chickens are our choice at the restaurant. They are cooped in a traditional way, but fed natural feed and are growth-hormone free. This more controlled raising process yields a bird that is consistent in size, full flavored, and remarkably tender. One thing we don't use is frozen birds. The freezing process can compromise

a lot of flavor and juices. Although it seems strange, it can be very difficult to find fresh chickens in the average market. You pick up a fryer and it is thawed yet has been frozen at one time. This is due to the limited shelf life of chicken and the need for modern food chains to avoid loss. As with anything ask questions and stick with a meat purveyor that understands your demand for quality.

Game hens is really a euphemism. At one point there were chicken strains that followed the lineage of Cornish hens, but modern production needs have cast this aside in favor of today's modern, fast-growing strains of chicken. Most commercially available game hens are really just young chickens. Do not let this fact devaluate them in your cooking repertoire. These tender young birds are flavorful and make a great presentation. My favorite way to go is to debone the carcass, stuff it, and roast it.

Chiles

Pablano, or *pasilla, chilies* are one of our most favorite at the restaurant. We always roast them and peel the outer skin then do everything from stuffing them to chopping them up for salsa or using the sweet and spicy flavor in soups and sauces.

Jalapeño peppers are often used in a way that they overpower the core of a dish, but this does not have to be the case. In America we tend to lean to the more-is-better way of cooking and more jalapeños can mean that the end product is just too spicy. Like many other flavor ingredients there are ways to get the best out of a jalapeño without allowing it to be overwhelming. The first method is to roast the pepper over open flame and peel the outer skin. Remove the seeds and rinse the remaining roasted flesh, and of course use them in moderation. Jalapeños can also take on a life of their own by smoking after the roasting process (in this form they are known as chipoltes).

Habenaros can be absurdly hot and need to be treated with great respect. Do not, however, let their power keep you from using them. When used properly and in moderation they have a pleasant heat and a good ability to boost other flavors in your dish.

Anaheim chilies grow readily in Idaho and have a mild heat and sweet flavor. They are a great choice for roasting and stuffing. Often I find the flavor of Anaheims lends well to stuffing with shellfish like lobster or shrimp. If you have a backyard garden in Idaho, this is a rewarding crop to grow since they do well in our summer heat and tend to produce a bumper crop.

Corn

As early as late June to late September on a good year corn grows generously on thousands of Idaho farms. Enjoying this crop can be as easy as boiling it, spreading it with butter, and eating it, or as far flung as fleecing the kernels off the cob and pureeing it for a simple sauce to accompany duck breast. No matter what you choose to do with it, you are enjoying yet another fruit from the miracle of irrigation. The water that we harvest from the snow-capped peaks every summer and divert to unlock the fertile volcanic soils of the Idaho desert makes the commercial corn harvest, as well as many others, possible.

Garlic

Whole clove garlic is an essential part of cooking. I rarely cook with garlic that is not roasted (see *Techniques*) because to me roasting leaves you with what is great about garlic while removing what is not. There are some small producers of garlic in Idaho; however, it seems the bulk of what we use is from eastern Washington or Gilroy, California. No matter the origin, look for firm bulbs that are not shriveled from outer husk and a nice white color to the husk, both good indicators of freshness. You'll also find that dedicating a little space of your garden rewards you with some of the finest garlic you've ever eaten because while garlic does keep well, it is best enjoyed fresh.

Herbs (fresh)

Basil is one of my favorite fresh herbs. From the sweet flavor of green leaves to the purple fragrance of opal basil, there are not many dishes it does not enhance. Another easy to produce item from your home garden, it is also readily available in most markets these days. At the restaurant we often use the stems in stocks to give them a backbone of sweet basil flavor.

Chervil is a hugely underused fresh herb and really can be used in a variety of ways. At the restaurant it is most commonly used as a last-minute ingredient tossed into a dish just prior to being served to add a taste of freshness. I also love to use the lacy leaves as a plate garnish.

Cilantro can be best described as having a very "alive" flavor. I like this herb best when it is at its freshest either in a salsa or tossed into a dish just before service. Cilantro can also make a great pesto, as well, when ground with roasted garlic and lime juice.

Dill has such a unique flavor and needs to be used sparingly so as to not overpower the other ingredients in a dish. I have never found a piece of fish that fresh dill does not go well with. I will also say that my favorite potato salad has a touch of chopped fresh dill as well.

Mint is a highly prolific cash crop in Idaho. The obvious flavor pairing for mint is with lamb. I like to incorporate copious amounts of fresh mint into the braising liquid with shanks or make a mint pesto to slather on grilled lamb. There are many uses and again you will find mint does well in your garden and produces almost year round.

Parsley is often thought of as merely a plate garnish. I find that parsley, like cilantro, can have a very fresh and alive flavor if added to a dish at the last minute. At the restaurant, we blend parsley into our greens for our house salad. When chopping parsley, be sure to place it in a clean cloth and squeeze some of the collagen out before introducing it to the dish. This process keeps the flavor fresh and your dish from turning green.

Rosemary is the most memorable of herbs. It has a flavor that always reminds me of riding my mountain bike through the pine forests of northern Idaho. It is a hearty grower that can bear usable product as many as ten months a year. It is also very sinewy and the leaves need to be either ground (I use a coffee grinder for this) or strained after imparting its flavor and before being served.

Sage is the essence of the desert. One of the most heavenly smells in the world is the smell of the sage in the desert after a rainstorm. Sage does well chopped and added to a dish, it can be fried, and it can used as a flavorful garnish or added to a stock and strained for essence. No matter how you use it, just use it. More than any other herb it is the flavor that says Idaho.

Thyme is my choice for a poultry herb. It does a great job of expanding the flavor profile of a chicken dish. It can be a bit of a task to pick the tiny leaves from the stem but it is well worth the effort. One way to get around the picking of the leaves is to wrap thyme, or any of the previously mentioned herbs, in cheesecloth and tie it with roast twine during the simmering process. Just pick the cloth out prior to serving.

Honey

There are many clover honey producers in Idaho and just over the hill from Boise in Emmett are several of the best. The unique thing about honey from southern Idaho is that it has a subtle taste of sage. I assume this is a result of the fact that foraging for pollen is inevitably going to run a bee into sage. At the restaurant honey is a culinary cure-all. If the sauce is too bitter, add a little honey and so on. All too often people reach for the sugar when honey would make more of an impact.

Lamb

Shanks are one of my favorite dishes to cook. Because they take such a long time, they are easily infused with a myriad of flavors. The best shanks for long braising times are hind shanks. They have a larger calf muscle and tend to hold together better during a 3-hour cook time. The shank can be difficult to sever from the top of the leg, and this is something you probably want to have done for you at the butcher counter.

Rack of lamb is the definitive cut in fine dining restaurants. The real beauty of the lamb raised in Idaho is that the racks have a very large eye, especially when you compare it to that of the imported lamb from Australia and New Zealand. There are a number of ways that you can go about preparing racks but I think the real key is to not cook them much past medium-rare since there is very little fat marbled into the eye to carry it to a well-done.

Sirloin of lamb, like beef, is a hugely underrated cut. It is intensely flavorful and juicy. It takes a little more care during the preparation process and is often best carved against the grain when served. Don't pass up this gem of a cut, since it is probably the best value you can find in a piece of lamb.

Mushrooms

Morel is the king mushroom in the state of Idaho. The availability of this mushroom has us a bit jaded at times, since we tend to forget they can sell for as much as 75 dollars a pound in New York City. There are not many dishes the morel's delicate flavor and exquisite texture won't enhance. At the restaurant during the season (late April to July in a good year) we simmer them in dry sherry cream for a simple appetizer. They are best found on the slopes of pine forests throughout Idaho.

Watch out for the morels that grow in the marshy snow-melt bogs since they often contain ringworms and grubs inside their caps.

Like morels, *chanterelles* are a fleeting and seasonal delicacy. This mushroom sometimes appears in the spring if the conditions are right, but their real season is from when the rains start in the fall until the first snows. There are several different strains and all are good if they are harvested while firm and not mushy. They make a great accompaniment to any braised meat, fish, or poultry dish and have a distinct yet subtle flavor.

Shiitake mushrooms have a natural nutty flavor that works well to enhance the other flavors in a dish. They need to be used a little sparingly since they can overpower. There are small pockets of forest in Idaho where wild shiitakes can be found; however, shiitakes lose little in the translation to domestic cultivation and are readily available. When using shiitakes be sure to remove the sinewy stem.

Oyster mushrooms are rather prolific on the rotting stumps of trees in many Idaho forests. The oyster mushrooms we use in the restaurant are cultivated in an abandoned mine near Twin Falls and are as large, flavorful, and beautiful as any I have ever seen.

Onions

Chives have such a tender and delicate flavor that they can be used in many different ways. One of our primary uses for chives at the restaurant is for garnish. They can be sliced fine to sprinkle the rim of a plate or cut in lengths to provide elevation to a plate by sticking them out of mashed potatoes or the like.

Shallots are delicate little onions with a sweet flavor that just can't be duplicated. As you can tell by the recipes in this book, they are a large part of our repertoire at the restaurant. Their most common use is for a flavoring ingredient in sauce reductions like *beurre blanc,* but they can also be used as delicate little "onion rings" for a garnish. Experiment with shallots in place of onion in different recipes and you will be amazed at the difference.

Bermuda onions, or red onions, can be too powerful for a lot of applications. Often I like to temper their power by roasting them. This yields a much more relaxed and sweet flavor. For dishes like *ceviche* and certain salsas ,the raw flavor of a Bermuda onion may be welcome. When adding Bermuda onions to these items don't overdue it since the flavor "grows" over time.

Yellow onions are grown throughout Idaho. Many are kin to the famous Walla Walla sweet, made famous in a town just several hours down Interstate 84 from Boise. I use these onions liberally in the restaurant. My favorite use is in a ragout that I place under a steak or roast. I also like to make onion marmalade out of them by slow roasting them with the juice and zest of oranges.

Leeks are also a favorite at the restaurant. Their uses are many. I always try to use the whole leek by using the bottom white part in a sauté and then pureeing the greens into an asparagus soup to extract both the sweet flavor and rich green color. However you choose to use leeks, make sure to slice them and then rinse them to remove all the soil. The layers trap the sandy, moist soil they grow in and ruin a dish if not rinsed properly.

Partridge

Hungarian partridge, or "Huns," as they are referred to are prolific in the high-desert sage fields of Idaho. Because these birds are quite small, they are best plucked and roasted whole. They can be breasted and used that way; however, it takes several hunters' limits to provide enough breasts for a dinner for four.

Polenta (cornmeal)

Because we produce so much corn in Idaho, cornmeal is also a staple. I have learned that different grades of meal (coarse, medium, or fine) in different ratios to each other produce different textures of polenta, and experimenting with these ratios is well worth the time involved. Cornmeal, however, is not simply about polenta. Simply seasoning a piece of catfish and coating it with cornmeal and then frying it crisp can achieve a simple crispy coating. Don't forget about its potential in breads and desserts as well.

Potatoes

Russet Burbank potatoes are the gem of Idaho. They grow large and flavorful in the irrigated volcanic soil. In this book and at the restaurant there are varied uses for this Idaho staple. I always buy them in unsorted sizes and then pick out the different sizes for different uses. The price is very low when you buy them this way. So low, in fact, that it is difficult to think of a better value in any other type of food.

Red potatoes are also a favorite at the restaurant. They do well mashed with their skins or can be carved for an elegant presentation. I also use these potatoes to make cakes that are the foundation for a number of our meat and fish presentations.

Yukon gold potatoes have a rich gold color in their flesh. They have a sweet flavor and are one of my favorite potatoes to roast. They are becoming increasingly available in markets and make a great addition to the backyard garden as well.

French fingerling potatoes are fun to use because of their unique shape and petite size. I like to use them whole in soups and stews. They have a sweet earthy flavor and an incredibly silky texture.

Peruvian purple potatoes have a fun visual appeal as well. They are a cross strain of red potatoes and beets that occurred in the farms of South America where crop rotation and sterility are not so carefully practiced. As kin to the beet, they are sweet and strikingly purple especially inside. A little vinegar in the water during the boiling process helps to maintain their rich color.

Quail

There are several species of quail that inhabit Idaho. Every morning I watch the quail feed in my backyard as I have my coffee. They are a delicate bird but tasty when treated properly. Because they are rather small in stature, I usually bone the carcass, then stuff and roast them. Lately, boned quail have turned up on the market, and this is an attractive alternative since they can be difficult to bone yourself. If you hunt your own, I recommend at least three days' hanging prior to plucking and cooking.

Steelhead

Often misconstrued as a salmon, steelhead are actually ocean-going trout. In the cold winter months anglers try their hand at this elusive catch. Ten years ago it was not entirely uncommon to see steelhead in the fish markets from time to time. This has become almost completely unheard of these days and really the only way to taste this fish is to be or know an angler. While there are subtle differences the recipes in this book that call for steelhead can be replaced with salmon filet with no ill effect.

Tomatoes

Roma tomatoes are the most frequently used at the restaurant. We like them because they are generally easy to find ripe almost year-round and they have a high content of flesh versus seed, which makes them better for smoking or roasting.

Green zebra tomatoes are grown in southern Idaho with great success. They are green with yellowish stripes, which gives them great eye appeal, and are as richer in tomato flavor than any of their red counterparts.

Grape tomatoes have become our favorite choice for salads in the past year. They have grown well in my garden and are the first to ripen, as tasty and sweet as anything, and have a deep red color. We simply slice them in half and throw them on top of our salads.

Yellow teardrop tomatoes are a fleeting treat in the late summer. The yellow color always makes it difficult to anticipate their incredibly rich tomato flavor. I love to make yellow tomato sauce out of them just for something different. While the yield of these plants is not stellar, it is worth planting a plant or two just to achieve something different out of your garden.

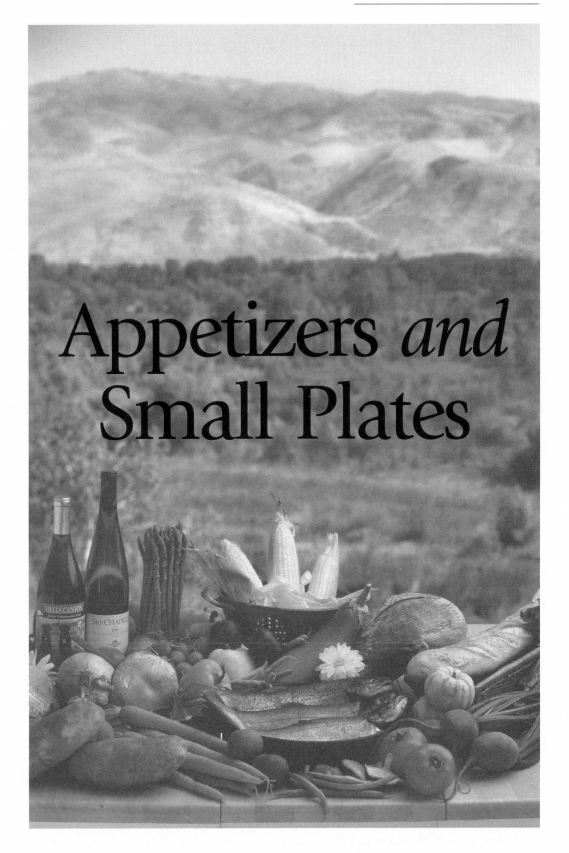

Appetizers *and* Small Plates

Crisp Polenta with Roasted Peppers and Mozzarella

Yield: 8 servings

I have always found that it's best to use a mixture of cornmeal textures to make perfect polenta. The mixture I use is about 75 percent fine and 25 percent course cornmeal. The purpose of this is to give the finished product a richer texture. This also aids in the firmness of the finished product.

For the polenta:

2 quarts chicken stock

½ cup coarse ground cornmeal plus additional for dusting

1½ cups fine ground cornmeal + ½ cup for coating

salt to taste

1 teaspoon ground cumin

½ teaspoon cayenne pepper

1 roasted red pepper, seeded, stemmed, and julienne

1 cup grated mozzarella cheese

1 tablespoon fresh basil leaves, very fine julienne

1 quart canola oil

■ Spray a nonstick muffin tin with corn oil spray and set aside. Bring the stock, cumin, cayenne, and salt to a boil. Combine the two cornmeals and slowly pour into the boiling stock in a steady stream while stirring constantly with a wooden polenta spoon or a stiff whisk. Be sure to add the polenta slowly and stir vigorously to avoid lumps. Lower heat and continue to cook and stir for an additional 3 minutes. Check the salt level one last time and remove from the heat. Fill the prepared muffin tins with half the prepared cornmeal. Distribute the mozzarella, basil, and roasted peppers amongst the polentas, in their centers, cover with the remaining polenta, and pack it firm with a spoon. Set the polenta aside to cool completely (about 2 hours).

Heat the canola oil in a large, thick skillet to about 350 degrees. (If it is smoking, it is too hot. If you place the polenta in the pan it should immediately sizzle.) Coat the prepared stuffed polentas with the residual fine cornmeal and carefully place in the hot oil. Cook for 1 minute or until they start to brown; then carefully flip them over and repeat the process. Remove them from the pan and place them on a cooling rack to allow any excess oil to drain. If needed, they may be held in a warm oven for up to 5 minutes while you prepare to serve them.

■ Heat the oil in a saucepan over medium heat and sauté the ingredients, stirring frequently. Blend ingredients until smooth.

To serve: Center 1 ounce of sauce on a warmed plate. Place a piece of the polenta on top of the sauce and garnish with basil leaves.

For the smoked tomato sauce:

4 ripe red tomatoes, cut in half, seasoned, and smoked

1 tablespoon olive oil

4 fresh basil leaves

1 tablespoon roasted garlic

½ teaspoon fresh ground black pepper

kosher salt to taste

2 tablespoons tomato paste

Pickled Button Mushrooms with Smoked Salmon

Yield: 12 portions, or 36 mushrooms

Choose mushrooms that are large for this dish since they shrink during the blanching process. Cold-smoked salmon works best for this dish and a presliced product may be easier to handle.

For the mushrooms:

▪ Remove the stems from the mushrooms and rinse the caps. Heat the olive oil in a pan and sauté the mushroom caps and garlic cloves for 2 minutes being careful not to brown the garlic. Add the white wine to the pan. Reduce the heat and place a lid on the pan. Cook the mushrooms for 3 minutes or until they are soft and cooked through. Remove the mushrooms from the heat and strain any excess liquid. Put the mushrooms and garlic in a glass jar or bowl and combine the remaining ingredients. Place the mushrooms in a refrigerator for 24 to 48 hours prior to use.

36 large button mushrooms

2 tablespoons olive oil

1 cup white wine

6 garlic cloves, peeled

1 cup white wine

1 cup water

1 tablespoon fresh dill sprigs

2 teaspoons kosher salt

10 whole black peppercorns

3 bay leaves

½ oz. caviar (Beluga or Osetra)

very thin tomato and lemon slices for garnish

To stuff the mushrooms:

▪ Place the mushroom caps, bottom up, on a work surface and fill each with approximately ½ teaspoon sour cream. Cut each slice of salmon into three pieces and twist the pieces into a rose shape and plug them gently into the mushrooms. Garnish the salmon roses with a sprig of dill and 6 to 8 eggs of caviar.

To serve: Arrange the mushrooms on a tray garnished with tomato and lemon slices.

12 ½-ounce slices cold smoked salmon

¼ cup sour cream

36 small fresh dill sprigs

½ ounce caviar (optional)

Grilled Eggplant in Spicy Tomato Marinade with Goat Cheese

Yield: 6 appetizer portions

When selecting your eggplants, be sure they are firm and free from bruises. If you attempt this recipe with soft eggplant, you will find it all but disintegrates by the time the dish is complete.

For the eggplant:

2 large eggplants

2 tablespoons roasted garlic puree

3 tablespoons extra virgin olive oil

sea salt

fresh ground black pepper

■ Preheat grill to medium-hot temperature. Remove the skin from the eggplant with a paring knife and slice it into ½-inch-thick planks. Combine the garlic with the oil and coat the slices of eggplant with the mixture. Season with salt and pepper and place the eggplant on an oiled grill. Cook for about 1 minute on each side or until the eggplant softens. Get some nice grill marks on the eggplant, but don't let it blacken at all. Remove the eggplant from the grill and place it in a shallow glass dish suitable for marinating and set aside to cool.

For the marinade:

4 ripe Roma tomatoes

2 tablespoons olive oil

sea salt

fresh ground black pepper

½ cup white wine vinegar

1 pablano chili, roasted, peeled, and seeded

3 fresh basil leaves, fine julienne

■ Preheat oven to 400 degrees. Core the tomatoes and coat with the olive oil and sprinkle with fresh ground sea salt and black pepper. Place the tomatoes in a roasting pan and place in the oven for 15 minutes. Remove the tomatoes from the oven and allow to cool. Peel the skin off the tomato and discard it. Place the tomatoes with any remaining juices and oil from the pan in a blender with the chili, vinegar, and basil. Process until smooth then toss it with the grilled eggplant and allow it to sit overnight in the refrigerator.

To serve: Serve the eggplant with 3 to 4 ounces of crumbled mild goat cheese *(fromage blanc)* sprinkled over the top.

Smoked Chicken and
Idaho Morel Mushroom Crepes

Yield: 12 portions (12 crepes)

From spring to midsummer on a good year, you can find fresh morel mushrooms in the pine forests of Idaho. Make sure to educate yourself thoroughly prior to picking your own wild mushrooms. Also be sure to slice the mushrooms and rinse them prior to use, inspecting the cavities for parasites.

Specialty groceries sometimes carry these delicate mushrooms but often at a premium price. If all you can find is dried morels be sure to reconstitute them in warm water for 10 minutes, then drain them and gently press any additional water from them prior to starting the crepe filling. I like to keep the mushroom broth that comes from reconstituting dried mushrooms and replace the stock or broth called for in a recipe with the rich mushroom broth.

For the crepe batter:

1 cup all-purpose flour

2/3 cup whole milk

2/3 cup water

3 large eggs

6 tablespoons clarified butter

■ Place the milk, water, and eggs in a mixing bowl and beat vigorously. Slowly sift in the flour while continuing to whisk, then whisk in 3 tablespoons of the clarified butter. Strain, then refrigerate the mixture for 1 hour.

Heat a nonstick 6- to 8-inch pan over medium heat until medium hot then coat with ½ teaspoon of the clarified butter. Add 1 ounce of the batter and spread evenly around the bottom of the pan. Cook until the crepe is formed and flip the crepe with a high heat rubber spatula. Remove the crepe from the pan and repeat the process with the remaining 11 crepes. Separate the crepes with wax or parchment paper until needed.

▪ In a 4-quart saucepan heat the butter and sauté the shallots until they are translucent. Add the chicken and continue to sauté for an additional 2 minutes. Add the cream and the stock and season with the salt and pepper. Taste and adjust with more salt and pepper if needed. Cook for 3 to 5 minutes then add the sliced morels.

Strain the morels and the chicken off the sauce and return the sauce to the pan. Place the chicken and mushrooms in a glass bowl with plastic wrap over it so it can be reheated in a microwave when it is time to stuff the crepes. Bring the sauce back to a boil on the stove and slowly whisk in the dissolved cornstarch until the sauce resembles a thin gravy. Add the fresh thyme leaves to the sauce and keep warm until the crepes are ready to serve.

To assemble the crepes: Place a crepe on a work surface. After rewarming the stuffing place about 3 ounces across the center of the crepe. Roll the crepe and place it on a warm entrée sized plate (one crepe is sufficient for an appetizer, but two make a nice entrée). Ladle about 2 ounces of the sauce over the crepe and sprinkle with chopped parsley or garnish with a sprig of the fresh thyme and serve.

For the stuffing:

12-ounce smoked chicken breast, cut thin julienne

1 tablespoon chopped shallots

2 teaspoons butter

1 cup heavy cream

1 cup chicken stock

2 cups sliced morel mushrooms

½ teaspoon salt

¼ teaspoon ground white pepper

½ teaspoon fresh thyme leaves (dried is okay if fresh is not available)

1 teaspoon cornstarch dissolved in water

fresh thyme sprig and/or chopped parsley for garnish

Idaho Potato and Smoked Trout Cakes

Yield: 12 portions (approximately 24 2-ounce cakes)

Use a healthy, large, russet potato for the base of this cake. The potato can be microwaved until cooked through as opposed to being baked.

Make sure the small strip of pin bones is removed from the trout filet prior to introducing to the cake batter.

For the cakes:

½ pound smoked trout

1 pound Idaho russet potatoes

2 egg whites

1 teaspoon salt

½ teaspoon fresh ground black pepper

¼ cup fine sliced green onions

2-cups fine breadcrumbs

½ red bell pepper, diced very fine

1 cup canola oil

dill sprig or chopped parsley for garnish

■ Wash the potatoes and prick the tops with a fork. Bake the potatoes in a 400-degree oven for 45 minutes or until tender all the way through. Allow to cool slightly then cut the potatoes in half lengthwise and grate the flesh down to the skin. Dice the smoked trout in small pieces and add to the potatoes (discard the skin) with the green onions, egg whites, and red bell pepper. Combine ingredients thoroughly. Add salt and pepper to taste.

Form the cakes in 2-ounce rounds that are approximately 2 inches in diameter and ¾ of an inch thick. Heat the canola oil in a nonstick skillet over medium heat and pack the cakes with breadcrumbs just prior to placing them in the skillet. Allow to cook until golden brown on one side (about 90 seconds) then flip and repeat on the other side. Place the cakes on paper towels to drain any excess oil. The cakes can be kept warm in a 200-degree oven for up to 15 minutes prior to service.

For the tarter sauce:

■ Combine the ingredients in a food processor until smooth and refrigerate for 2 hours prior to use.

To serve: For a sit-down meal shingle two of the cakes in the center of a warm entrée plate. Place the tarter sauce in a squeeze bottle and lay a zigzag pattern of the sauce over the cakes and garnish the plate with a wedge of lemon and a sprig of fresh herb, preferably dill or flat leaf parsley. Or arrange on a tray for a buffet with a dish of the tarter sauce in the center.

1 cup mayonnaise

1 lemon, zested

1 tablespoon lemon juice

½ teaspoon turmeric

10 to 12 capers, chopped fine

¼ teaspoon salt

¼ teaspoon fresh ground black pepper

1 teaspoon chopped fresh dill

1 teaspoon fresh garlic clove, chopped very fine

Spicy Catfish Potstickers with Orange Soy Sauce

Yield: 32 potstickers

This savory Asian dumpling makes an outstanding appetizer and is good either hot or cold. Catfish filets make a great filling for this but if you have bass or trout you can easily substitute either for the catfish.

For the potstickers:

10-ounce catfish filet, fat trimmed

1 teaspoon minced fresh garlic

1 tablespoon grated ginger root

1 teaspoon oyster sauce

1 teaspoon chopped fresh cilantro

3-ounce can water chestnuts

1 jalapeño, stemmed, seeded, and chopped fine

32 wonton wrappers

½ cup peanut oil

½ cup water

1 egg, mixed with 1 teaspoon water

corn starch for dusting

■ Chop the catfish into 1-inch pieces and place in a food processor. Add the garlic, ginger, cilantro, water chestnuts, oyster sauce, and jalapeño. Pulse the machine 6 to 8 times or until the mixture is rough-chopped and combined. Lay the wonton wrappers out on a work surface and place approximately ½ ounce of filling at the bottom left corner of each wrapper. Use a pastry brush to paint the edge of the wrappers with the egg and water mixture. Fold the wrappers from the top right corner to the bottom left corner forming a triangle. Place the potsticker on the work surface with the point of the triangle pointing up. Press down slightly to form a flat bottom and crimp the seams with your fingers. Place the potstickers on a corn starch-dusted plate to avoid sticking.

Cook the potstickers by heating the oil in a skillet and placing the flat side of the potsticker down. Cook for 1 minute or until the base begins to brown. Pour the water in the pan and cover with a lid. Cook for an additional 3 minutes.

■ Combine ingredients and allow to steep for several hours at room temperature.

To serve: Remove potstickers from the pan and place on a warmed plate. On the side, serve a dish of the orange soy sauce. Garnish with sprigs of cilantro.

For the sauce:

juice and zest of 1 orange

½ cup soy sauce

10 cilantro leaves

additional cilantro sprigs for garnish

Trout Fritters with Corn Relish

Yield: 12 portions (about 36 fritters)

It is always best to use trout that is fresh caught, but today's advances in aquiculture have afforded us a few alternatives. Many trout farms freeze their fish within minutes of being harvested and cleaned. This is a much better product for this dish than a 4- or 5-day-old "fresh" fish.

For the fritters:

4 boned 10- to 12-ounce Idaho rainbow, brown, or cutthroat trout

1 cup fine ground cornmeal

1 teaspoon salt

½ teaspoon fresh ground black pepper

1 cup buttermilk

zest and juice of 1 lemon

2 cups canola oil

■ Clean the trout filets off the skin by sliding a knife under the filet while pulling on the skin. Cut the ridge of pin bones out of the filet (you can feel the pin bones by running your finger along the filet). Cut the filets in four or five 1-ounce pieces and toss with the lemon juice in a glass bowl. In a shallow dish combine the cornmeal, lemon zest, salt, and pepper. After the trout has sat in the lemon juice for 5 minutes, pour the buttermilk into the bowl with the trout and coat the pieces of trout thoroughly. One at a time, coat the pieces of trout with the cornmeal breading and place them on a plate or tray so they are not touching.

Heat the oil in a skillet to 375 degrees. Place the trout fritters in the skillet one at a time until the skillet is full. Cook for 45 seconds then flip and cook on the other side. Remove the fritters from the oil and place on a paper towel–lined plate to drain any excess oil and repeat the process with the remaining fritters. Keep the fritters warm in a 200-degree oven for up to 15 minutes prior to service.

Bring 2 quarts of water to a boil and place the tomatillos in the pot. Reduce the heat and place a lid on the pot. Allow the tomatillos to cook for 5 minutes then strain the water off and place the tomatillos in a food processor. Process the tomatillos until they are a smooth puree (about 2 minutes). Place the tomatillo puree in a bowl and allow to cool. Cut the corn off the cob and combine with the tomatillos and the remaining ingredients. Taste and adjust with more salt and pepper if needed. Allow the mixture to sit refrigerated for at least 4 hours prior to service.

To serve: Place the fritters on a tray with a bowl of the corn relish in the center. Garnish with reserved sprigs of cilantro.

For the relish:

1 large ear fresh corn, husk removed

6 tomatillos, husk and stem removed

1 jalapeño, stem and seed removed, chopped fine

2 teaspoons ground cumin

1 teaspoon salt

½ teaspoon fresh ground black pepper

1 teaspoon fresh garlic, minced

1 tablespoon fresh cilantro, chopped, plus extra sprigs for garnish

juice and zest of 1 lime

Soups *and* Salads

Two-Toned Roasted Pepper Soup

Yield: 8 servings

Since this soup is all about the peppers, it is important that you select sweet fresh ones. A few things to look for are smooth skins that are free from dimples and blemishes. I find that the thicker the flesh is, generally the sweeter it is. While you can usually find red and yellow peppers year-round it is best to use fresh local ones from mid- to late summer.

■ Coat the bell peppers with olive oil and char on the grill. Place in a paper bag until cooled. When cooled, peel off the charred skin and remove the core and seeds and rinse in cold water. Remove the skin from the onion, slice in half and then julienne. Heat 1 tablespoon butter over medium in each of two separate stock/saucepans. Divide the onions between the two pans and cook until translucent. Add the red peppers to one pan and the yellow peppers to the other pan. Cook for 2 minutes. Add half the stock to each pan and add the turmeric to the yellow pepper pan and the paprika to the red pepper pan. Cook the soups for 10 minutes at a low boil and whisk in 1 cup cream and add three basil leaves into each pan. Puree the soups with an immersion blender until smooth. Bring the two soups back to a low boil and slowly whisk in half the dissolved cornstarch mixture into each pan. Cook for 2 more minutes, then season with kosher salt. Strain each soup and return to each pan to warm for service.

To serve: Place the soup into different pitchers and pour 4 ounces of the yellow pepper soup on the lefthand side of a soup bowl and finish with 4 ounces of red pepper soup poured on the right side of the bowl. Be careful not to jiggle the bowls too much so as to maintain the two-toned coloration of the soups. Garnish with chopped chives if desired.

2 red bell peppers
2 yellow bell peppers
1 ounce olive oil
2 tablespoons unsalted butter
1 large Vidalia onion
5 cups chicken broth
2 cups heavy cream
1½ teaspoons ground turmeric
2 teaspoons Hungarian paprika
6 fresh basil leaves
kosher salt to taste
2 tablespoons cornstarch dissolved in water
1 tablespoon chopped chive

Banana Squash Soup

Yield: 6 servings

Banana squashes can get very large, and I have found that as they get bigger, they get sweeter. A 20-pound banana squash, however, can be a lot more than you need. Recently I have seen 2- and 3-pound chunks available in some markets and this can be a much more practical way to go. If you do end up with a whole squash, try steaming the flesh until soft and then pureeing. At that point you can freeze the puree in appropriate portions and save until needed. Try substituting banana squash puree for pumpkin in a pie recipe; it's delicious.

■ Heat the olive oil in a soup pan and cook the onion until translucent, but do not allow the onion to brown. Add the banana squash and chicken stock and bring to a boil. Cover the pan, reduce the heat, and allow to cook for 20 minutes or until the squash is soft. Puree the soup with an immersion blender or in a blender. Season with the white pepper, nutmeg, and salt.

To serve: Strain the soup through a fine sauce strainer, then stir in the heavy cream and serve in bowls.

2 pounds peeled and seeded banana squash, cut into 1-inch chunks

2 quarts chicken stock

½ white onion, diced fine

1 tablespoon olive oil

½ teaspoon ground white pepper

½ teaspoon ground nutmeg

kosher salt to taste

1 cup heavy cream

Summer Corn Soup with Roasted Peppers

Yield: 6 servings

This soup is only as great as the corn you use. The variety of corn is not as important as the quality. Look for crisp, sweet kernels.

In a stockpot combine the chicken broth, water, corncob, and leek tops and bottom. Bring to a boil and reduce heat to a simmer. Cover and cook for 1 hour. Strain broth and set aside. In a soup pan melt the butter, and sauté the shallot, shiitake mushrooms, and leek until soft. Sprinkle the flour over the mixture and cook for 1 minute, stirring constantly. Add the previously made stock to the pan with the potatoes and whisk to combine. Bring the mixture to a boil and reduce the heat to a simmer. Allow the soup to cook for 5 minutes then add the corn, diced roasted pepper, heavy cream, black pepper, and salt and leave on the heat until the ingredients are warm but the corn is still crisp.

To serve: Ladle the soup into warm bowls and sprinkle with the chopped parsley.

2 ears fresh corn (kernels removed, cob reserved)

1 quart chicken broth

1 cup water

1 leek, tops and bottom removed and reserved, center sliced thinly

6 large shiitake mushrooms, stems removed, julienne

1 roasted red pepper, diced fine

1 shallot, peeled and diced fine

2 tablespoons butter

2 tablespoons flour

2 cups heavy cream

2 small white potatoes, diced fine

1 teaspoon fresh ground black pepper

kosher salt to taste

chopped parsley for garnish

Tomato Beef Stew with Pearl Barley

Yield: 6 servings

In Idaho we grow some of the best pearl barley in the world. When cooked properly, it takes on the flavors of what it is cooked with. The very best way to cook barley and not make your dish too starchy, is to boil the barley separately until it is cooked al dente, rinse the barley in cold water to remove excess starch, then finish it with the components of your dish.

■ In a saucepan combine the barley and water with approximately 1 teaspoon of salt and bring to a boil. Cook the barley for 30 minutes on a slow boil or until the grain is cooked, but still has texture. Place the barley in a strainer, rinse with cold water, and set aside. In a stockpot heat the vegetable oil over medium heat. Season the meat with salt and pepper and coat lightly with the flour. Sauté the meat in the oil until browned, then strain the oil from the pan and return the meat and pan back to the heat. Add the garlic, onion, celery, and carrot and continue to cook for 2 more minutes stirring frequently over medium-low heat being careful not to burn the garlic.

Add the red wine then add the stock, tomatoes, potatoes, bay leaves, thyme, and rosemary. Cook the stew for 60 minutes at a simmer with a lid on to tenderize the meat. Stir in the tomato paste and the cooked barley and continue cooking with the lid on at a low simmer for an additional 5 minutes, or until the barley is completely tender.

To serve: Remove the bay leaves. Ladle the soup into warm bowls and serve with a slice of fresh bread.

3 pounds beef chuck roast or sirloin, fat removed, then meat diced in 1-inch cubes

flour for dusting

1 tablespoon vegetable oil

½ yellow peeled onion, diced into ½-inch pieces

6 stalks celery, cut on the bias

2 carrots, peeled, halved lengthwise, and cut on the bias

1 tablespoon chopped fresh garlic

2 bay leaves

½ teaspoon dried thyme

½ teaspoon fresh rosemary leaves, chopped very fine

1 cup dry red wine

3 cups beef stock

6 medium red potatoes, quartered

2 tomatoes, cored and diced in ½-inch pieces

½ cup tomato paste

salt and fresh ground black pepper to taste

1 cup pearl barley

1 quart cold water

Smoked Salmon Chowder with Potato and Leek Terrine

Yield: 6 servings

For this chowder I like either an alder or hickory "hot" smoked salmon (cooked through not just "cured"). This chowder also requires a good stock, but the truth is that salmon bones don't make the best stock. The best way around this is to ask the fishmonger for white fish bones when you are getting the smoked salmon. Make a stock out of them by placing the bones in a stockpot with some carrot, celery, and onion, covering with cold water, and adding about a tablespoon of pickling spice for each gallon of water. Boil for 90 minutes occasionally skimming the foam and impurities that come to the surface. When done strain the stock through a chinoix or fine sauce strainer. If this is too overwhelming, substitute clam juice for the fish stock.

For the chowder:

■ In a 2-gallon stockpot melt the butter over medium-high heat and add the onion, celery, carrot, and garlic. Sauté for 3 to 5 minutes stirring frequently until the vegetables are translucent but not at all brown. Add the flour and stir constantly for 1 minute to incorporate. Add the fish stock and whisk thoroughly to incorporate the flour mixture. Bring the mixture to a boil and reduce the heat to a simmer. Cook for 5 minutes, then add the herbs and pepper and season with the sea salt. Just prior to service stir in the heavy cream and crumble in the salmon.

1 pound smoked salmon

3 tablespoons butter

2 stalks celery, diced fine

1 carrot, peeled and diced fine

1 small white onion, peeled and diced fine

1 teaspoon roasted garlic

½ cup flour

6 cups white fish stock

½ teaspoon fresh thyme, plus sprigs for garnish

½ teaspoon fresh oregano

1 teaspoon fresh ground black pepper

sea salt to taste

1 cup heavy cream

■ Salt the water, bring to a boil over high heat, and add the diced red potato. Cook for 3 minutes or until soft, strain, and set aside. In a nonstick sauté pan melt the butter and add the leeks. Cook until the leeks are soft, but not at all brown. Combine the potatoes into the leeks and season with the black pepper and salt to taste.

To serve: Pack the potato into a small (2-ounce) ice cream scoop and unmold into the center of a warm bowl. Ladle the chowder around it and garnish with thyme sprig if desired.

For the terrine:

3 red potatoes, 1/4-inch dice

1 leek, top green and bottom removed, halved, and fine julienne

2 quarts cold water

kosher salt to taste

1 tablespoon butter

¼ teaspoon fresh ground black pepper

Grilled Lamb Salad

Yield: 12 entrée-sized salads

It is best to buy spring lamb. A boned leg should be no larger than 3 pounds. If the boned leg is larger than 3 pounds, the meat may have a gamier flavor and be more fatty. Buy the roast from a reputable meat merchant. Have the leg boned and trimmed to 1/8-inch fat on the outside. If your butcher is able to tie the lamb leg for you then you are able to save a step later. Fresh Malabar spinach is used for this dish and is found in most specialty and chain grocery stores in the spring since it grows very well in Idaho. If you are unable to find Malabar spinach, any fresh spinach with stems on will do. Spinach grows in sandy conditions and needs to be rinsed thoroughly and stems removed prior to using.

For the lamb:

2½ to 3 pounds boned lamb leg

1 ounce virgin olive oil

1 tablespoon fresh garlic cloves, peeled and sliced

2 tablespoons fresh rosemary leaves

1 teaspoon dried lavender

2 teaspoons fresh ground black pepper

1 tablespoon kosher salt

▪ Tie the boned lamb leg with string at least three times around the center of the leg. Combine the garlic, salt, pepper, lavender, rosemary, and olive oil and coat the lamb leg thoroughly. Place the lamb leg on a roast rack in a roasting pan and place in a 500-degree oven for 10 to 12 minutes until lamb leg begins to brown. Reduce heat to 225 degrees and cook for another 1 to 1½ hours according to how well done you want your lamb. Use a meat thermometer to check the center of the roast for doneness. As a guide, 130 degrees in the center is medium-rare—warmed through but still pink in the middle. A thermometer temperature of 140 to 145 degrees is medium-done—no longer pink in the middle, but the meat is still juicy. Above 145 degrees is medium-well to well.

Remove the roast from the oven and have it rest for 10 minutes prior to carving.

■ Combine all ingredients except the oil in a food processor or electric mixer bowl and blend for 30 seconds. With the motor running, slowly drizzle in the canola oil until combined. Place the completed dressing in a glass bowl or container and refrigerate until needed.

For the dressing:

2 tablespoons Dijon mustard

½ teaspoon fresh rosemary leaves

fresh basil leaves

½ teaspoon dried thyme

3 tablespoons white wine vinegar

2 teaspoons minced fresh garlic

1 teaspoon lemon juice

1 egg yolk

1 teaspoon kosher salt

½ teaspoon fresh ground black pepper

1 cup canola oil

To assemble the salad:

To serve: Toss the spinach in the dressing and divide evenly among 12 chilled entrée-size plates. Pile the spinach in the center of the plates. Carve the lamb leg in half-inch slices and place approximately 4 to 6 ounces of lamb on each salad. Garnish with the tomato and cucumber and serve.

1 pound 4 ounces fresh spinach leaves

12 wedges tomato (Or use cherry tomatoes, cut in half.)

12 cucumber rounds, ¼-inch thick sliced

1 prepared lamb leg roast

1½ cups dressing

Exotic Green Salad
with Huckleberry Vinaigrette

Yield: 8 entrée-sized portions, or 12 first-course portions

Use crisp-looking, whole head lettuces. Always peel lettuce away from the core by hand since a knife will bruise the lettuce and cause the edges to brown. Make sure to soak the leaves thoroughly and remove the greens from the sink instead of allowing the water to drain. That way, the greens won't come into contact with any sand or dirt that has sunk to the bottom of the sink. It is very important to use a salad spinner since the dressing adheres much better to dry leaves.

For the vinaigrette:

■ Combine all ingredients, except the oil, in a food processor. Run processor for 45 seconds to combine ingredients. While the motor is running, drizzle in the olive oil until totally blended. Refrigerate until needed.

1 cup fresh huckleberries (Use frozen if fresh are unavailable.)

3 tablespoons raspberry flavored vinegar

1 teaspoon chopped fresh garlic

2 teaspoons Dijon mustard

4 fresh basil leaves

1 egg yolk

1 teaspoon salt

½ teaspoon fresh ground black pepper

1 cup olive oil

For the greens:

■ Tear leaves from core and rinse well in a sink of cold water. Place rinsed leaves in a salad spinner, spin thoroughly, and place the greens in a large salad bowl.

To serve: Toss greens in 1 cup of the raspberry vinaigrette. Divide and place a tuft of dressed greens into the center of chilled entrée or salad plates as necessary.

1 head bib lettuce

1 head radicchio

1 head curly endive

24 leaves mustard or horseradish greens

Grilled Tomato Salad

Yield: 8 salad-course portions

This is a fabulous salad for late summer and early fall when your backyard garden has yielded an excess of tomatoes. It is a nice dish for vegetarians since it has a grilled flavor without any meat. Make sure the tomatoes are large, ripe, and firm, since soft tomatoes may not hold their shape during grilling.

For the tomatoes:

■ Core and slice the tomatoes into half-inch slices. Place the tomatoes in a large bowl and toss with the remaining ingredients. Place the tomatoes on a preheated grill and cook for approximately 90 seconds on each side or until the tomatoes start to soften. Remove the tomatoes to a plate and refrigerate until ready to use.

4 large, vine-ripened tomatoes
2 tablespoons olive oil
2 teaspoons kosher salt
1 teaspoon fresh ground black pepper

For the dressing:

■ Combine the ingredients and refrigerate until ready to use.

3 tablespoons balsamic vinegar
½ cup olive oil
8 basil leaves, cut julienne
½ teaspoon fresh ground black pepper
½ teaspoon kosher salt
1 teaspoon chopped fresh garlic

To assemble the salad:

1 red onion
grilled tomato slices
balsamic vinaigrette dressing
exotic salad greens optional

■ Peel the skin off the onion and slice paper thin while keeping the rings of the individual onion slices intact. Toss the onions with the dressing to coat. In another bowl toss the tomato slices with dressing.

To serve: Arrange the tomato and onion slices on a chilled salad plate and serve. If desired, a tuft of greens can also be tossed in dressing and served with the tomato and onion slices.

Idaho Trout Bisque

Yield: 8 servings

When too many trout are caught to eat fresh within a day, freeze extra trout to make this soup. If trout are unavailable, catfish, bass, or virtually any white meat fish works well is this soup.

■ Clean the trout filets off the skin and remove the rigid pin bone from the trout by slicing out that section with a sharp filet knife. Dice the trout into ½-inch pieces. Set aside. Rough-chop the tomatoes into 1-inch pieces and set aside. In a stockpot, heat the oil and add the leeks and garlic. Sauté for 3 to 5 minutes on medium heat until the leeks become translucent. Be careful not to brown the garlic. Add the tomatoes and continue cooking for another 5 minutes, stirring frequently. Add the sherry to the pan and cook for 2 more minutes. When finished cooking, puree the soup—preferably with an immersion blender—until smooth and return the soup to a low boil. Season the trout with salt and black pepper. Add the trout, fish stock, and dill, and cook for 5 minutes. Add the cream and bring back to a boil. While at a low boil whisk in the tomato paste and cream and allow to simmer for 5 minutes. Check the bisque for seasoning and add salt and pepper to taste.

To serve: Place 8 ounces of soup in warmed soup bowls and garnish with sprigs of fresh dill. At the restaurant we often serve this with a crouton of toasted baguette bread topped with a slice of melted Brie cheese.

2 rainbow or brook trout, approximately 10 ounces each

1 leek, sliced lengthwise, then ¼-inch sliced

4 vine-ripened large tomatoes

1 teaspoon garlic

1 tablespoon olive oil

½ teaspoon fresh ground black pepper

kosher salt to taste

2 tablespoons chopped fresh dill

1 cup dry sherry

2 cups heavy cream

4 cups white fish stock

¼ cup tomato paste

sprigs of fresh dill

Jicama Salad with Orange Cumin Dressing

Yield: 8 servings

Brought to Idaho by Mexican immigrants, jicama is a vegetable that grows much like a potato. Generally, the larger the jicama, the sweeter it is.

■ Peel the rough outer skin on the jicama with a paring knife. Slice into ¼-inch-thick slices, stack, and slice again into ¼-inch pieces. The pieces should have a matchstick shape when finished. Peel the carrot and slice it like the jicama to achieve the same matchstick shape. Julienne the red onion and bell peppers discarding stems and seeds. Combine the vegetables in a bowl. Pull the cilantro leaves off their stems and add to the bowl. Add the remaining ingredients and toss well. Refrigerate at least a half hour prior to service.

To serve: Line a chilled salad plate with leaf lettuce and place approximately 6 ounces of the salad on top of the lettuce. Garnish with a lime wedge for squeezing.

1 large jicama
½ bunch cilantro
½ red onion
1 red bell pepper
1 yellow bell pepper
1 medium to large carrot
juice and zest of 1 large orange
1 tablespoon white wine vinegar
1 tablespoon olive oil
1 teaspoon cumin
½ teaspoon fresh ground black pepper
1 teaspoon kosher salt
1 head leaf lettuce
1 lime cut in 8 leaves

Pumpkin, Idaho Potato, and Leek Soup with Hot Sweet Pumpkin Seeds

Yield: 8 servings

This soup is adapted from a dish popular in Northern Spain called Porusalda and is inspired by the large Basque population around Boise. If pumpkin isn't available, banana, butternut, or acorn squash can be substituted.

For the soup:

½ teaspoon nutmeg

2 leeks

6 cups water

3 Idaho russet potatoes, peeled and chopped into 1-inch pieces

1 small pumpkin (about 3 to 4 pounds)

1 teaspoon fresh ground black pepper

salt to taste

3 tablespoons cold pressed extra virgin olive oil

1 tablespoon chopped parsley

■ Cut the top and the bottom off the pumpkin and remove the rind. Cut the pumpkin in half, spoon the seeds out, and set aside for the garnish. Cut the bottom inch off the leeks. Slice the leeks in half lengthwise and rinse in cold water separating the layers and making sure to remove any dirt (place the leeks in a strainer and rinse with cold water if necessary). Chop the leeks into ¼-inch sections and place in a stockpot with the potatoes, pumpkin, and water, and bring to a low boil. Cover and cook for 45 minutes. Whisk the soup with a wire whisk to lightly break up the potatoes and pumpkin. Season the soup with pepper, salt, chopped parsley, and nutmeg.

For the spicy pumpkin seeds:

1 cup pumpkin seeds
¼ teaspoon cayenne pepper
¼ teaspoon cumin
1 teaspoon kosher salt
½ teaspoon ground white pepper
1 teaspoon sugar

■ Preheat oven to 300 degrees. Combine the cayenne, cumin, salt, white pepper, and sugar and set aside. Place 1 quart cold water in a stockpot and bring to a boil. Make sure the pumpkin seeds are rinsed free of any pumpkin pulp and place them in the boiling water for 3 minutes. Strain the seeds and shake off any additional water. Shake the spice mixture on the seeds and place them on a baking sheet. Bake the seeds in the preheated oven for 20 minutes or until they start to brown.

To serve: Ladle 8 ounces of soup into warmed soup bowls or hollowed-out, rinsed, and warmed baby pumpkins. Drizzle each bowl with 1 teaspoon of the olive oil and garnish with the toasted pumpkin seeds.

Lemon Chicken Soup

Yield: 8 servings

While most Americans prefer the breast of a chicken, I find that the back of the bird (legs and thighs) contain more flavor and have a much nicer texture for dishes like soups and stews. Another bonus is that these cuts of chicken can cost as much as half as much as breast meat. When selecting shiitake mushrooms, make sure the skin is soft. Don't purchase any that are leathery or dry.

■ Peel and finely mince the shallots. Remove and throw away any shiitake mushroom stems, then slice the mushrooms into ¼-inch julienne slices. Heat the oil over medium-low heat in a small stockpot and add the minced shallots. Cook until the shallots are translucent and then add the chicken and cook until the meat is seared on all sides. Add the mushrooms and flour and cook for another 2 minutes. Whisk in the stock and bring the soup to a low boil. Add the cream, turmeric, lemon juice, and zest and whisk thoroughly. Adjust the flavor with salt as necessary.

To serve: Ladle 8 ounces of the soup into warmed soup bowls and garnish with chives. At the restaurant we like to strain the chicken and the mushrooms from the broth and form it in a small ramekin that we unmold in the center of the bowl. We then ladle the broth around the terrine of chicken and mushrooms. Although this is not entirely necessary, it makes a lovely presentation.

1 pound raw chicken thigh meat, cut into ¼-inch pieces

2 whole shallots

1 ounce olive oil

8 to 10 large shiitake mushrooms

6 cups warm chicken stock

1 cup heavy cream

2 tablespoons all-purpose flour

2 ounces lemon juice

2 tablespoons lemon zest

kosher salt to taste

1 teaspoon turmeric

3 tablespoons chives cut into 2-inch long sections

Smoked Chicken and Chanterelle Mushroom Soup

Yield: 8 servings

Chanterelle mushrooms grow in moist grassy bogs and pine forests throughout Northwestern Idaho from mid September until Thanksgiving in a good year. The lower stem of this mushroom is often quite tough and needs to be peeled or trimmed and discarded. Be sure not to overcook the mushrooms so they retain their luxurious texture. If you are unable to find fresh chanterelle mushrooms, many specialty grocers carry canned chanterelles from Europe.

For the soup:

1 whole smoked chicken

2 shallots skinned and chopped fine

½ pound chanterelle mushrooms

1 tablespoon butter

8 cups water

1 cup heavy cream

1 onion coarsely chopped

8 black peppercorns

2 tablespoons cornstarch, dissolved in water

salt and fresh ground black pepper, to taste

chopped fresh parsley

■ Pull the chicken meat from the carcass. Place the bones, chicken skin, onion, peppercorns, and water in a large stockpot. Bring to a boil and reduce heat to low. Cook uncovered for 1½ hours. Strain the stock into a glass bowl and skim all fat from the top. Rinse the pot and return it to the burner. Melt the butter and sauté the shallot until they become translucent. Add the chicken and cook for 2 more minutes. Return the stock to the pan and cook for 10 minutes. During this time rinse the mushrooms and tear them into quarters. Add the mushrooms, then the cream to the pot. Season with salt to taste. While cooking the soup at a low boil, slowly whisk in the cornstarch mixture to thicken the soup. Cook for approximately 2 more minutes.

To serve: Ladle 8 ounces of soup into warmed soup bowls and garnish with chopped parsley if desired.

Wild Mushroom and Sherry Soup

Yield: 8 servings

This recipe calls for oyster and shiitake mushrooms but when available chanterelle, morel, or crimini mushrooms make great soup also. In a pinch, when nothing else is available, this soup will work with domestic mushrooms but you might want to slightly increase the amount of mushrooms since the flavor won't be as intense as that of wild mushrooms.

For the soup:

1 leek

1-ounce shiitake mushrooms, sliced and stem removed

2-ounce oyster mushrooms, cut in half with the bottom part of the stem removed

2 tablespoons butter

1 teaspoon chopped fresh garlic

2 cups dry sherry

4 cups chicken stock

2 cups heavy cream

½ cup flour

1 teaspoon fresh ground black pepper

kosher salt to taste

chopped chive or edible flower petals

■ Chop the top 3 inches and bottom 2 inches off the leek and discard. Slice the leek in half lengthwise and cut into 1/8-inch slices. Place the sliced leek into a strainer and rinse thoroughly, being careful to remove all dirt. In a stockpot, heat the butter at medium heat and sauté the garlic for 45 seconds stirring frequently. Add the leek and mushrooms and sauté for 3 minutes until the leeks soften. Lower the heat and sift in the flour. Stir frequently so the flour does not burn. In another pot, heat the stock and sherry to a boil. Slowly whisk the hot stock and sherry into the leek, mushroom flour mixture and continue to stir for 2 minutes while the soup cooks. Whisk in the heavy cream and season with black pepper and kosher salt. Bring the soup back up to a low boil and simmer for 5 minutes to combine the flavors.

To serve: Ladle 8 ounces of soup into warmed soup bowls and garnish with chopped chive and/or edible flour petals.

Wilted Spinach Salad with Clover Honey and Bacon Dressing

Yield: 4 servings

The dressing for this salad is only as good as the bacon. Applewood smoked bacon is preferable as its sweet smoke flavor works well with the honey.

For the dressing:

■ Chop bacon into ¼-inch pieces and place in 4-quart saucepan. Cook over medium to low heat for 20 minutes, stirring frequently, until the bacon is completely browned. Strain the fat off the bacon and return the bacon bits to the pan. Add the shallots to the pan and cook for 1 minute. Add the vinegar, water, and honey and bring to a boil, then slowly whisk in the cornstarch mixture. Allow to cook at a low boil for 1 minute.

4 strips bacon
1 shallot, diced fine
½ cup red wine vinegar
½ cup water
3 tablespoons clover honey
1 teaspoon cornstarch dissolved in water

For the salad:

■ Preheat oven to 350 degrees. In a sauté pan bring the water and sugar mixture to a boil. Add the nuts to this mixture then toss and strain the excess liquid off. Return the nuts to the pan and toss with the cumin and cayenne pepper. Bake in the oven for 5 minutes, toss, and bake for an additional 5 minutes. Lay the nuts out on a sheet pan or plate to cool.

To serve: In a mixing bowl toss the spinach with the dressing and distribute onto four plates. Arrange the orange, tomato, carrot, and nuts over the spinach and serve.

4 cups spinach leaves, cleaned and stemmed
½ cup prepared honey bacon dressing, warmed
½ cup filets of orange
½ cup diced tomato
½ carrot, fine julienne
½ cup spicy candied hazel nuts (see below)

For the hazel nuts:

½ cup hazel nuts, unsalted
¼ cup sugar dissolved in ¼ cup water
¼ teaspoon cayenne pepper
½ teaspoon ground cumin seed

Fish

Cedar Plank Roasted Salmon with Mushroom Stuffing and Cucumber, Caper, and Dill Sauce

Yield: 4 servings

In Idaho it is always easy to get a good piece of salmon. With the proliferation of airfreight, fresh fish is only several hours removed from the coast. While it is easy to find wild salmon from spring to fall, farm-raised salmon (mostly out of British Columbia) is available year-round. You can buy cedar-roasting planks at most upscale culinary stores. It is also possible to use standard planks, but be absolutely sure they have not been chemically treated in any way.

For the salmon:

4 6- to 8-ounce boneless and skinless salmon filets

1 to 2 teaspoons kosher salt

1 teaspoon ground white pepper

1 cup fine julienne wild mushrooms (Earthier varieties, such as oyster, hedgehog, or chanterelle are best.)

1 shallot, chopped fine

¼ pound butter

■ In a sauté pan melt 2 teaspoons of butter then add the shallot. Cook for 2 minutes or so until they become soft and translucent. Add the mushrooms and cook over medium heat for 5 minutes. Season with salt and white pepper to taste and set aside to cool. Cut a horizontal slit in the skin side of the salmon filets and stuff with the mushroom stuffing. Place the filets on the roasting plank, stuffing side down, and season the tops of the filets with salt and ground white pepper and place a flake of butter on each filet. Place the planks in a 400-degree oven and cook for 12 to 14 minutes. I prefer the fish to be medium-rare or still somewhat translucent inside; however, you can adjust the cooking time to accommodate your own taste.

■ Combine the cucumber, dill, capers, sour cream, black pepper, and celery salt in a food processor and blend until smooth. Season with kosher salt to taste. Warm the sauce slowly and gently in a nonreactive saucepan; do not boil or leave on the heat too long or the sauce discolors and separates.

To serve: Place a 2-ounce pool of sauce on a warm plate and place the salmon filet over the sauce. Serve with wild or steamed white rice if desired.

For the sauce:

1 large cucumber, peeled and seeded

1 tablespoon capers

1 tablespoon chopped fresh dill

¼ cup sour cream

½ teaspoon celery salt

½ teaspoon fresh ground black pepper

kosher salt to taste

Soy-Glazed Salmon with Wasabi Mashed Potatoes and Thai Vegetable Slaw

Yield: 6 servings

Great vegetables really make this dish come alive. Make sure the colors are vibrant and the flesh firm. If certain vegetables are more in season than others don't be afraid to make substitutions.

For the slaw:

1 small cucumber, peeled, cut in half, and seeded

1 yellow squash

1 medium carrot, peeled, top removed

2 shiitake mushrooms, stem removed

½ red bell pepper, fine julienne

1 ounce ginger root, peeled and very fine julienne

¼ cup rice wine vinegar

1 teaspoon sugar

1 teaspoon kosher salt

16 to 18 cilantro leaves

1 teaspoon sesame oil

¼ teaspoon crushed red pepper flakes

■ Using a mandolin, process the cucumber, carrot, and the yellow squash in long, thin julienne. In a bowl combine all ingredients, cover, and refrigerate for at least 2 hours prior to service.

For the potatoes:

8 to 10 small red potatoes

1 tablespoon butter

¼ cup heavy cream

1 plus ½ teaspoon kosher salt

1 tablespoon wasabi powder

■ In a 4-quart saucepan bring 2 quarts of cold water and ½ teaspoon salt to a boil. Slice the potatoes in ½ inch-thick pieces and add to the water. Boil for 10 to 12 minutes or until the potatoes break easily when touched by a fork. Strain the water off the potatoes and place them in an electric mixing bowl. With a whisk attachment beat the potatoes until smooth then add the remaining ingredients and whip for an additional 30 seconds.

For the salmon:

▪ Place the broth in a pan with the salmon filets. Cover the filets with half of the soy glaze and place in a 400-degree oven. Allow to bake for 12 to 15 minutes or until just barely cooked through (slightly opaque in the middle). Remove from the oven and coat the filets with the rest of the honey soy glaze.

6 salmon filets (6-ounce), boneless and skinless

½ cup honey soy glaze (recipe below)

2 cups fish stock (Or use canned clam juice.)

For the honey soy glaze:

▪ Combine all ingredients in a saucepan except the cornstarch and bring to a boil. Reduce the heat and allow to simmer for 10 minutes. Bring the mixture back to a boil and whisk in the cornstarch solution. Pass the glaze through a strainer and allow to cool slightly before using.

To serve: Place ¾ cup of the mashed potatoes in the center of 6 warm plates and place the salmon filets on top of the mashed potatoes. Garnish the salmon with the Thai slaw on top and serve.

½ cup soy sauce

2 tablespoons honey

1 cup rice wine vinegar

1 ounce gingerroot

1 teaspoon sesame oil

1 teaspoon roasted garlic

12 cilantro leaves

1 tablespoon cornstarch dissolved in water

Rainbow Trout Roulade with Crisp Potato Cake

Yield: 4 servings

You can always find both great trout and potatoes in Idaho, but don't think that you don't have to be choosy. As always make sure the trout smells like the river and not fishy. With the advent of modern processing techniques you can even buy boneless and skinless filets of trout, which is what you need for this dish.

For the cake:

■ Wash and bake the potatoes at 350 degrees for 50 minutes or until cooked through. Remove the potatoes from the oven and allow to cool for 20 minutes. Cut the potatoes in half lengthwise and grate the white meat out of the skin into a mixing bowl and combine with the shallot, dill, salt, black pepper, and egg whites. Pack the batter into 4-ounce balls and press on a counter into ¾ inch thick cakes. Coat the cakes with cornmeal. In a nonstick pan heat the oil until it is hot, but not smoking. Cook the cakes for 1 minute or until golden brown, flip the cakes and place the pan in the oven for 3 to 4 minutes or until the other side is golden brown. Remove the cakes from the pan and blot with a paper towel in preparation for service.

2 large russet potatoes

1 tablespoon chopped shallot

1 teaspoon chopped fresh dill

kosher salt to taste

½ teaspoon fresh ground black pepper

2 egg whites

1 cup cornmeal

1 cup canola oil

For the trout:

■ Preheat oven to 400 degrees and butter an 8-inch square baking dish. In a nonstick sauté pan heat 2 tablespoons of the butter and add the shallots. Sauté for 45 seconds or until the shallots become translucent. Add the crawfish tail meat and cook briefly. Once the crawfish tails begin to turn red, toss with the spinach, dill, ½ tsp. salt, and ¼ white pepper, and remove the stuffing from the pan into a bowl.

Locate and remove the pin bones from the trout by making a slice on the top and the bottom of the row of bones and pulling the strip out with your fingers—most respectable fish markets will do this for you. Use a flexible filet knife to slide

4 8-ounce rainbow trout, head off and gutted

2 cups fresh spinach leaves

½ pound crawfish tail meat (Substitute rock shrimp if not available.)

1 tablespoon shallots, diced extremely fine

2 tablespoons plus 2 teaspoons butter

1 teaspoon kosher salt

½ teaspoon fresh ground white pepper

2 teaspoons fresh dill, chopped fine

1 cup white wine

the filet off of the skin. After the skin is removed from the four trout, place the filets two on top of each other each in four stacks, skin side up on a work surface. Sprinkle the filets with the remaining kosher salt and white pepper. Divide the spinach and crawfish stuffing into four even piles and place them in the center of the stacks of trout filets. Roll the two ends of the filets around the filling and secure the ends of the filets with toothpicks. Place the stuffed trout in the greased baking dish so that the stuffing is showing on the top and the bottom. Pour ¼ cup of the wine and a small flake of the remaining butter over each roulade and bake for 12 to 15 minutes or until the crawfish tails are just barely cooked through.

For the sauce:

1 cup dry white wine

juice of 1 lemon

zest of ½ lemon

¼ cup heavy cream

½ pound cold unsalted butter, cut into ½-ounce flakes

1 tablespoon chopped shallots

½ teaspoon chopped fresh dill

ground sea salt to taste

■ In a nonreactive (stainless steel or copper) saucepan combine the wine, lemon juice, and shallots. Bring the pan to a rolling boil and allow the mixture to reduce by ½ before whisking in the cream. Reduce the pan to a simmer and allow to reduce until the bubbles are thick and the reduction is the viscosity of maple syrup. With the mixture at a simmer whisk in the butter one flake at a time, waiting for one to dissolve prior to adding the next. Once all the butter is added whisk in the lemon zest and dill, remove from the heat immediately, and keep warm until service; I often hold it in a Thermos.

To serve: Place the potato cakes in the center of a warm plate and place the trout roulade stuffing side up on top of the potato cake. Pour 2 ounces of the sauce over the trout and garnish with a wedge of lemon and a sprig of dill.

Potato Crusted Steelhead Filets over Ratatouille

Yield: 6 servings

This dish works best with at least a 1-inch-thick filet. The reason is that this allows the fish to not be overcooked in the time that it takes to brown and crisp the potatoes. Because steelhead is often hard to come by, feel free to substitute salmon filets that are readily available year-round. I often serve this dish in a shallow bowl to hold the juices of the ratatouille with the potato crusted steelhead filet on top.

For the steelhead:

6 7-ounce steelhead filets

2 tablespoons canola oil

3 large russet potatoes, peeled and julienne

salt and fresh ground black pepper

2 eggs

½ cup milk

flour for dusting

■ Add the canola oil to a skillet and preheat over medium heat. Make sure the oil is hot, but does not smoke. Whisk together the eggs and the milk. Season the steelhead filets with the salt and pepper and dust with the flour, dip in the egg mixture, and pack the top with the potato. Place the salmon potato side down in the oil. Cook until the potatoes are golden brown without disturbing the salmon (about 3½ minutes). Flip and cook for 1 more minute or until the fish is just barely cooked through.

For the ratatouille:

1 cup tomato, chopped

1 cup zucchini and yellow squash, chopped

1 teaspoon chopped fresh dill

8 chanterelle mushrooms ripped in half

¼ cup salmon stock

¼ cup dry white wine

salt and pepper to taste

2 teaspoons butter

1 teaspoon chopped shallots

■ In a sauté pan, heat the butter and blanch the shallots. Add the tomatoes, mushrooms and squash/zucchini and cook for 2 minutes stirring often. Add the stock and white wine and cook until the tomatoes and squash are soft (about 10 minutes). Season with dill, salt, and pepper.

To serve: Distribute the ratatouille with broth into 6 warm bowls. Perch the completed salmon, potato crust side up, on top of the ratatouille and serve.

Poultry *and* Fowl

Artichoke Braised Chicken

Yield: 2 servings

This dish is best when the chicken sides are cooked with the skin intact. An easy way to prepare this from a whole chicken is to set a 3-pound frying chicken face-up on a cutting board. Use a boning knife to slice alongside each breastbone down the backbone of the carcass. Peel each side to the backbone and slice the skin on each side. Make a slice down the leg and thigh and carefully remove the bones from the flesh. Rinse the two sides in cold water and pat dry.

■ Heat the olive oil in a sauté pan. Season the chicken breast with salt and pepper and dredge in flour being careful not to knock off any excess. Place the chicken breast in the pan, skin side down, on medium heat and cook 90 seconds or until the skin turns golden brown. Flip the chicken breast and cook an additional 60 seconds. Remove the chicken from the pan and pour off any excess grease. Return the chicken to the pan (and heat) and add shallots and cook for 15 seconds. Deglaze the pan with wine and add the thyme, artichokes, tomato, mushrooms, and stock and swirl the pan to combine ingredients. Place the pan in a 400-degree oven and complete cooking for 15 to 17 minutes, or until the chicken is cooked through.

To serve: Remove the chicken from the pan and place each side on warm plates. Place the pan on a medium heat to reduce and thicken the sauce. Ladle the sauce and vegetables over the chicken and serve with steamed rice.

2 sides of chicken, carcass removed

salt and pepper

1 cup flour

12 artichoke heart quarters

1 large tomato cored and diced fine

1 cup wild mushrooms (Use oyster, chanterelle, or morel.)

1 cup white wine

1 cup chicken stock

2 ounce blended olive oil

2 shallots chopped fine

½ teaspoon fresh thyme leaves

Traditional Chicken Cacciatore

Yield: 6 servings

I learned this particular recipe on a foray to northern Italy. It was on this trip that I realized that most Americans have an unusual idea of what authentic Italian cuisine really is. Breast meat just won't do for this dish; you need legs and thighs. The advantage to this is that they are inexpensive and more flavorful.

■ Preheat oven to 375 degrees. In a large, oven-safe sauté pan, heat the canola oil to 350 degrees. Season the chicken with the salt and pepper and coat with the flour. Place the chicken in the pan and fry for 3 minutes on each side or until it has a golden brown crust. Remove the chicken from the pan and blot any excess oil off with a paper towel and set aside. Remove the canola oil from the pan and place it back on the burner on medium heat. Add the olive oil to the pan and quickly sauté the garlic and onion for one minute stirring constantly. Add the celery, carrot, and mushrooms, and continue to cook for 3 or 4 minutes, stirring frequently until the vegetables soften. Add the tomatoes, white wine, and chicken stock, bringing the mixture to a boil. Remove the pan from the heat and return the chicken. Place the pan in the oven for approximately 20 minutes or until the juices run clear when the meat is pierced.

To serve: In warm bowls place ½ cup of cooked pasta or risotto. Place a leg and a thigh over each. The sauce should be brothy and flavorful. If it has over-reduced add some stock, adjust the flavor with salt and pepper as needed, and swirl in the fresh basil then ladle over the chicken.

6 chicken leg and thigh sections, severed

flour for dusting

2 cups canola oil

1 tablespoon olive oil

kosher salt

fresh ground black pepper

1 tablespoon roasted garlic

½ yellow onion, diced very fine

1 stalk celery, diced very fine

1 small carrot, peeled and diced very fine

½ cup sliced mushrooms (Use porcini if you can get them.)

3 large tomatoes, cored and ½-inch diced

1 cup dry white wine

2 cups chicken stock

3 fresh basil leaves, fine julienne

Braised Game Hen with Corn and Tomatoes

Yield: 4 servings

Unfortunately, it is difficult to find game hens that are not frozen. This fact should not deter you from using them, since they do freeze well and lose little of their juice, but with this recipe it really won't be missed much. The thing that makes this dish special is the corn. Generally from late June to mid-August roadside stands filled with corn abound. I find that the flavor pinnacle of this crop is to be found by doing no more than heating the corn and not actually cooking it at all.

For the hens:

4 12- to 14-ounce game hens

3 tablespoons blended olive oil

1 tablespoon kosher salt

1 teaspoon fresh ground black pepper

flour for dusting

1 tablespoon butter

2 ripe tomatoes, cored and diced

2 ears fresh corn, peeled, rinsed, and kernels cut off ear

4 fresh basil leaves, fine julienne

1 cup dry white wine

1 cup seasoned chicken stock

8 red potatoes, cut in half and blanched until just barely cooked through

■ Preheat oven to 350 degrees. Place one of the game hens breast side down on a cutting board. Sever the wingtips leaving the short wing and make an incision on the lefthand side of the backbone. Continue to make slices along the carcass severing the thighbone from the carcass when you come to it. When you get to the breastbone fold the side of the hen that is removed from the carcass over the side that has not been and repeat the process from the first side backward.

This sounds complicated; however, after you have tried a few it gets easier. Finally, remove it by slicing along the thighbone and severing it from the leg, leaving the leg bone in tact. Make sure during this process to keep the skin in tact and when completed restore the bird to its original shape—albeit flat since it is missing its carcass. After you have completed this process on all four birds, season them thoroughly with the salt and pepper then dust with the flour. Heat a large skillet over medium heat with the olive oil. Place the hens in the skillet breast side down, making sure the skin completely covers all flesh. Keep the heat low enough so any residual flour in the pan does not burn.

After about 2 to 3 minutes the first side should be golden brown and they can be flipped and the process repeated on the other side. Remove the hens from the pan and pour the oil off. Place the pan back on the burner and deglaze the pan with white wine then add the chicken stock, potatoes, and tomatoes and return the game hens back to the pan. Place the pan in the oven and cook for 12 to 15 minutes or until just barely cooked through and juices run clear when the skin is pricked with a knife. Remove the pan from the oven and place the game hens in the center of four warm plates. Place the pan on a burner over high heat and add the corn kernels and basil. Allow to cook for 2 minutes over high heat while it reduces to the consistency of a broth soup.

To serve: Ladle the braisings over the chicken and enjoy.

Grilled Natural Chicken Breast with Asparagus Risotto

Yield: 6 servings

Great asparagus is everywhere in the spring. I prefer the early season asparagus which is about the same diameter as a pencil and the sweetest and most tender of the season.

For the marinade:

■ Combine all ingredients in a glass or ceramic dish large enough to lay the 6 chicken breasts flat.

½ cup lemon juice

1 tablespoon lemon zest

½ cup olive oil

3 fresh basil leaves, fine julienne

1 tablespoon fresh rosemary leaves

1 tablespoon fresh thyme leaves

2 teaspoons kosher salt

1 teaspoon fresh ground black pepper

For the chicken:

■ Preheat your grill to medium heat. Place a breast at the ten o'clock position on the grill and cook for 90 seconds. Move the breast to the two o'clock position and cook for an additional 90 seconds. This process gives you professional-looking diamond markings, which look great. Flip the breast and continue cooking until just barely cooked through.

6 8-ounce natural chicken breasts with short wing, marinated for 2 hours

■ In a sauté pan, heat the olive oil. Add the roasted garlic, leek, and sauté for 1 minute. Deglaze the pan with the white wine and add the arborio rice. Cook the rice for 2 minutes, tossing often. The rice may crackle a bit and this is fine, just be careful not to let the rice brown. Add 4 ounces of the warm chicken stock to the pan. Allow all the liquid to absorb then add 4 more ounces of stock to the pan. Continue to add the stock this way until all the liquid has been absorbed. Occasionally stir the rice to make sure the liquid is consistently absorbed. Add the asparagus and cook for one additional minute.

To serve: In six warm bowls, place 1/3 cup of the seasoned chicken stock. Place about 2/3 cup of the risotto on the chicken stock and then place the grilled chicken breast on top of the risotto.

For the risotto:

2 tablespoons blended olive oil

2 teaspoons roasted garlic puree

½ cup dry white wine

1 cup arborio rice

¼ cup red onion, diced very fine

2 cups chicken stock, kept at a simmer on the stove

¼ cup fine sliced leeks, rinsed carefully

¼ cup asparagus, cut on the bias in 1-inch sections

¼ cup fine-diced tomatoes, seeds removed

Chicken with Prosciutto and Fontina Cheese

Yield: 4 servings

Proscuitto is ham that is brined and dry aged as opposed to being smoked. There are no producers of this delicacy in Idaho that I know of. There are producers in Portland and Seattle. Some produce the Italian-style proscuitto and some produce the French-style jambon du pays. *The key to working with this style of ham is to slice it incredibly thin. In the restaurant, we have the luxury of a slicer to achieve this effect; however, a very sharp knife and a little patience can achieve a favorable result as well. Another detail that helps this dish is lightly pounding the breasts to a uniform depth to insure even cooking.*

■ Preheat oven to 375 degrees. Heat the oil in a large skillet and reduce the heat if it begins to smoke. Season the chicken with the salt and pepper and coat with flour. Place the chicken in the pan starting with the side the skin was removed from and cook for 90 seconds or until it is golden brown. Flip and repeat on the other side then remove the chicken from the pan and pour off the oil. Replace the pan on the heat, add the onion and bell pepper, and sauté for 2 minutes or until they soften. Deglaze the pan with the sherry, add the chicken stock and sage, and return the chicken to the pan. Top the chicken with the prosciutto and cheese and place in the oven for 10 to 12 minutes or until cooked through.

To serve: Place about 6 ounces of cooked pasta in four warm bowls and place the chicken breasts over the pasta. Reduce the sauce if too thin or add more stock if the sauce is too thick then ladle the sauce around the chicken.

4 6-ounce chicken breasts (boneless and skinless)

kosher salt to taste

fresh ground black pepper

flour for dusting

2 tablespoons blended olive oil

¼ cup thin sliced yellow onion (Use Walla Walla sweets if they are in season.)

½ red bell pepper, very fine julienne

½ cup dry sherry

½ cup chicken stock

5 to 6 fresh sage leaves, rough-chopped

8 slices proscuitto, sliced very thin

1 cup grated fontina cheese (Use grated mozzarella if fontina is not available.)

Tarragon Braised Chicken

Yield: 4 servings

Tarragon is one of those herbs that suffers minimal ill effects by being dried. This being said, however, you will definitely achieve your best results by using fresh tarragon when available in this dish.

■ Preheat oven to 350 degrees. Heat a medium-sized skillet with the olive oil over medium heat. If the pan starts to smoke reduce the heat. Season the chicken breasts with the salt and a few turns of a pepper grinder. Dust the breasts with flour tapping off any excess. Place the chicken in the skillet skin side down and cook until golden brown—about 90 seconds. Flip the breasts and repeat the process with the other side; then remove the breasts from the pan and carefully pour off the oil. Return the pan to the heat and add the shallots allowing them to sizzle for 30 seconds, then deglaze the pan with the white wine and the lemon juice. Whisk in the mustard, stock, and cream, then return the chicken to the pan skin side up. Place the pan in the oven and braise for about 20 minutes or until cooked through.

To serve: Place warm cooked risotto in four bowls and place the chicken on top. If the sauce is too thin reduce on the stove top. If the sauce is over-reduced, thin with a little chicken stock. Once the desired consistency is achieved, ladle the sauce over the chicken and garnish with sprigs of tarragon.

4 chicken breasts, short wing and skin on

1 tablespoon blended olive oil

flour for dusting

kosher salt to taste

fresh ground black pepper

20 fresh tarragon leaves stripped from stem (or ½ teaspoon crushed dry)

1 teaspoon strong Dijon-style mustard

1 teaspoon shallots, chopped fine

2 tablespoons dry white wine

1 teaspoon fresh lemon juice

1 cup chicken stock

1 cup heavy cream

Hungarian Partridge in Puffed Pastry

Yield: 12 servings

Morsels of Hungarian partridge, or "Huns," breast are used. These small delicate breasts cook rapidly so you need to avoid overcooking them. If your day finds you unable to hike miles of sage in search of this elusive bird, morsels of chicken breast or turkey can be substituted.

For the puffs:

■ Cut the puff pastry sheet into 3-inch rounds with a biscuit cutter or glass and remove the extra pastry. Place the rounds on a nonstick baking sheet. Score the center of the puff discs with a 2-inch biscuit cutter or glass. Place the pastry in a 350-degree oven for 10 minutes. Remove the pastry from the oven and brush with the egg mixture. Then sprinkle with the thyme leaves. Place the pastry back in the oven and cook for an additional 6 to 10 minutes or until the puffs are fully risen and golden brown. Allow the puffs to cool slightly and press the scored center of the puff in with your finger.

1 12-inch by 12-inch sheet prepared puff pastry (or equivalent-sized sheets)

1 egg whisked with 2 teaspoons water

1 teaspoon fresh thyme leaves

1 egg whisked with 1 tablespoon water

For the filling:

■ In a nonstick sauté pan, heat the oil. Cut the partridge breast into ½-inch pieces and season with salt and pepper. Add the shallots to the pan and cook for 30 seconds. Add the partridge and mushrooms and sauté for 1 minute or until the morsels are seared. Add the white wine and then the cream and bring to a simmer. Cook for 2 minutes and remove from the heat.

To serve: Warm the pastries briefly in the oven. Dish the partridge and mushrooms into the cavities of the puffed pastry using a slotted spoon. Spoon the remaining sauce over the top. Cut the chives into 2-inch sections and sprinkle over the pastries. Place the completed pastries on a tray garnished with fresh thyme or parsley sprigs and serve immediately.

12 ounces Hungarian partridge breast

1 large shallot, chopped fine

6 button mushrooms, scrubbed and sliced

1 cup heavy cream

1 ounce white wine

½ teaspoon salt

¼ teaspoon fresh ground black pepper

6 chives

2 tablespoons olive oil

12 thyme or parsley sprigs

Herb Roasted Duckling with Orange and Ginger Essence

Yield: 4 servings

You will need a good-sized (3½- to 4-pound) duckling for this dish. The best way to prepare a duck for roasting is to leave it in the refrigerator for a day or so to let the skin dry out a little. This gives you a crisper skin that does a better job of locking in the juices since it is less permeable when you roast it.

For the duckling:

■ Preheat oven to 450 degrees. Peel the onion and cut it in quarters. Cut the orange in quarters as well and stuff both the onion and the orange into the cavity of the carcass. With an 18-inch piece of roast twine, loop the middle around the wings, cross the two ends under the back, and tie them up around the legs. Coat the outside with the salt and pepper; then place the duckling in a roasting pan and top with the herbs. Place the duck in the oven for 15 minutes or until it begins to brown then reduce the heat of the oven to 350 degrees. Cook for about an hour and 15 minutes or until the juices run clear when the leg is pricked. Remove the duck from the pan and allow it to rest on a cutting board to rest for 5 minutes prior to carving.

1 large duckling

1 tablespoon coarse sea salt

½ teaspoon fresh ground black pepper

1- to 2 ounces fresh herb sprigs (Use thyme, rosemary, sage, chervil, and/or parsley.)

1 yellow onion

1 orange

For the orange and ginger essence:

■ Zest two of the oranges, being careful to only remove the orange skin and none of the white pith. Juice all six of the oranges and incorporate in a nonreactive saucepan with the ginger, honey, and vinegar. Reduce over medium heat being careful not to scorch the pan until reduced by two-thirds.

6 Valencia oranges

2-inch piece of ginger root, peeled and sliced into ¼ inch dice

3 tablespoons white wine vinegar

1 tablespoon honey

To serve: Remove the breast, leg, and thigh from the duckling. Slice the breast and sever the leg from the thigh. Place a small pool of the orange essence on four plates and arrange some of the breast meat with a leg or thigh on top of it. Serve with steamed vegetables and red potatoes.

Crisp Gingered Duck Breast with Soba Noodles

Yield: 6 servings

Duck breast is one of our biggest sellers at the restaurant and I can never get away from the Asian preparations. When buying domesticated duck look for Moscovy duck, since it is tender yet still flavorful. If you have an opportunity to hunt for mallards or the like, they work well with this recipe. After you breast them you can use the remaining carcass and hind quarters to yield the rich stock that makes the soba noodles so great.

For the duck breast:

6 boneless duck breasts, skin on

6 ounces gingerroot, peeled and sliced thin

½ cup rice wine vinegar

2 tablespoons soy sauce

1 clove roasted garlic, squeezed from husk

1 shoot lemongrass, sliced

½ teaspoon Thai chili paste

10 cilantro sprigs

½ cup peanut oil

½ cup fine ground cornmeal

¼ cup canola oil

■ Preheat oven to 400 degrees. Place the peeled and sliced ginger in a nonstick pan and roast in the oven for 12 minutes or until very fragrant. Place the roasted ginger in a marinating pan and add the vinegar, soy, garlic, lemongrass, chili paste, cilantro sprigs, and peanut oil and whisk together. Coat the duck breasts completely with the marinade and let them sit in the pan skin side up. Cover and refrigerate for at least 2 hours and not longer than 12 hours.

In a nonstick pan heat the canola oil over medium heat. Remove the duck breasts from the marinade and coat the skin side with the cornmeal. Place the breasts in the pan and cook for 2 minutes or until golden brown and crisp. Flip the breasts and place the pan in the oven to cook for 8 to 10 minutes or until the duck breast is between medium-rare and medium. Remove the breasts from the pan and allow resting for 2 to 3 minutes before carving.

■ Place the ginger in a 2-quart saucepan and place in the oven for 10 minutes or until fragrant. Remove the pan from the oven and add the stock, vinegar, chili paste, garlic, and soy sauce and bring the mixture to a boil on the stove. Reduce the heat to a simmer and cook for 2 minutes. Whisk in the cornstarch mixture and allow simmering for an additional minute. Add the tomato, scallion, cilantro, and noodles to the pan, and cook until heated through.

To serve: Distribute the noodles into 6 bowls and pour the broth over. Carve each breast into thin slices and fan out around the noodles. Garnish with cilantro sprigs.

For the noodles:

2 pounds cooked soba noodles

1 cup rich duck stock

2 tablespoons rice wine vinegar

1 tablespoon ginger, peeled and diced very fine

½ teaspoon Thai chili paste

1 teaspoon soy sauce

1 scallion, sliced on bias

1 tomato, 1/4-inch diced

12 cilantro leaves, stem removed

1 teaspoon roasted garlic puree

1 tablespoon cornstarch, dissolved in water

10-12 cilantro sprigs

Spicy Catfish Potstickers (page 38)

Idaho Potato and Smoked Trout Cakes (page 36)

Crisp Polenta with Roasted Peppers and Mozzarella (page 30)

Two-Toned Roasted Pepper Soup (page 44)

Wilted Spinach Salad (page 61)

Potato Crusted Steelhead Filet (page 70)

Rainbow Trout Roulade (page 68)

Potato and Chevre Tart (page 104)

Peppercorn Roasted Elk Loin (page 110)

Lavender Marinated Lamb Skewers (page 116)

Grilled Lamb Salad (page 50)

Roasted Leg of Lamb (page 114)

Vegetarian

Wild Mushroom Strudel

Yield: 20 appetizer-sized portions

From late fall through early winter, many different kinds of mushrooms are available. From one mushroom expert to the other, opinions differ as to whether or not it is a good idea to mix strains of mushrooms in a dish. To my knowledge mixing strains of mushrooms does not cause ill effect and greatly adds to the flavor complexity of this dish.

1 pound assorted mushrooms, stemmed if necessary and diced very fine

½ red onion, diced fine

1 ounce blended olive oil

1 cup dry red wine

1 tablespoon fresh tarragon leaves, stemmed and chopped

sea salt to taste

fresh ground black pepper to taste

2 tablespoons melted butter

1 package prepared filo dough

1 egg whipped with 1 teaspoon water

■ Preheat oven to 375 degrees. In a large sauté pan, heat the oil and cook the onion for 2 minutes, stirring frequently. Add the mushrooms and sauté for an additional 2 minutes. Add the red wine and tarragon and mix thoroughly. Allow the mixture to cook over medium heat for approximately 20 minutes, stirring occasionally. The mixture should cook until all visible liquid is reduced. Season the mixture with the salt and pepper and lay it out on a sheet pan to cool.

While the mushroom mixture is reducing, lay the filo dough out on a work surface and cut it in half lengthwise. Lay the two different dough sheets on individual pieces of parchment paper. Separate the layers of each half and paint with the butter. Once the mushroom mixture has cooled, distribute it into two batches and spread it over the two pieces of pastry leaving about 1 inch uncovered around the entire edge. Paint the exposed edge with the egg mixture. Using the parchment as a crutch tightly roll up the strudel. When completed place the strudels seam side down on a parchment-lined baking sheet. Bake for 20 to 25 minutes or until golden brown.

To serve: Allow the strudel to cool slightly then with a sharp serrated knife slice into 1-inch slices. Arrange the slices on a serving tray for presentation. Often I serve this with pureed beets since the earthy tones work well together.

Fresh Mozzarella Cheese in Herb Crust with Basil Coulis

Yield: 6 appetizer portions

There are a number of different ways producers pack fresh mozzarella. Buying the cheese shrink-wrapped rather than the brine attains the best quality. The brine can have a tendency to bleach the flavor from the cheese. If you do purchase the cheese in brine make sure that the ball of cheese is in tact and not in slices. This also prevents the bleaching of flavor.

For the cheese:

In a medium-sized skillet, heat the oil to 350 degrees. Season the cheese with salt and pepper. In a shallow pan combine the breadcrumbs with the thyme, rosemary, and sage. Coat the cheese thoroughly with the flour, then with the egg mixture, then roll it in the herbed breadcrumb mixture. Place the coated balls in the hot oil and cook for about 45 seconds or until golden then flip and repeat. Remove the cheese from the pan and blot any excess grease with a paper towel.

3 2-ounce balls fresh mozzarella cheese, cut in half

sea salt

fresh ground black pepper

1 teaspoon thyme leaves

½ teaspoon rosemary leaves, chopped very fine

2 fresh sage leaves, chopped very fine

2 cups breadcrumbs

flour for dusting

2 eggs, whipped with 1 tablespoon water

2 cups canola oil

For the coulis:

Combine all ingredients in a food processor or blender and puree until smooth. Pass the mixture through a medium-fine strainer

To serve: Place a small pool of the coulis on a plate and place a piece of the herb-crusted cheese on top. Garnish with any remaining sprigs of herbs.

1-cup basil leaves (stem removed)

Juice and zest of one lemon

3 tablespoons extra virgin olive oil

1 teaspoon roasted garlic puree

kosher salt to taste

fresh ground black pepper to taste

Roasted Garlic, Potato, and Chevre Tart

Yield: 10 portions (1 tart)

Goat's milk cheese or chevre is made by a number of small producers in Idaho. Local made cheeses are often available at specialty grocers although their availability can be seasonal. The best choice for this dish is fromage blanc, *a creamy, spreadable goat's milk cheese. Unlike many cheeses,* fromage blanc *is best with little aging. Aging goat's milk cheeses can often produce too strong a flavor.*

For the crust:

1 1/3 cup pastry flour

1½ ounces cold unsalted butter, cut into small flakes

1 teaspoon kosher salt

1 teaspoon fine chopped fresh basil

¼ cup ice water ▸

▪ Combine the flour, butter, and salt in a mixing bowl. With the dough hook attachment of an electric mixer, blend the ingredients until combined thoroughly. Add the basil and slowly drizzle in the water until the dough pulls into a ball (this may require more or less of the ice water than listed in the ingredients). Remove the dough, wrap in plastic, and refrigerate for 2 hours prior to rolling out.

Coat a work surface with a light dusting of flour and roll out the dough ball to 14 inches round and approximately ¼-inch thick. Use additional flour as necessary to avoid sticking. Fit the dough round into a 9–10 inch fluted edge tart pan and prick the crust bottom with a fork. Place foil over the bottom and up the sides of the crust. Fill the foil-covered shell with dried beans and bake for 20 minutes in 350-degree oven. Remove the beans and foil and return the crust to the oven to bake another 12 minutes or until golden brown. Let the crust cool.

For the garlic:

4 whole garlic cloves

2 tablespoons olive oil

½ teaspoon salt

½ teaspoon fresh ground black pepper

◼ Cut the top ½ inch of each garlic clove with a paring knife. Place the cloves cut ends up in a small baking dish. Pour ½ tablespoon of the olive oil over each clove and sprinkle with salt and pepper. Cover the dish with foil and bake in a 300-degree oven for 1 hour. Remove the pan from the oven and allow to sit for a half hour before removing the foil.

For the potatoes:

2 large russet Burbank potatoes

1 ounce butter

3 tablespoons sour cream

½ teaspoon fresh ground black pepper

salt to taste

◼ Peel and rough-chop the potatoes and boil until cooked through. Strain the potatoes and place in a bowl and mix until smooth. Add the butter and sour cream and combine thoroughly. Season with salt and pepper to taste. Keep warm until ready to assemble the tart.

To assemble the tart:

½ cup *fromage blanc*

4 cloves roasted garlic

whipped potatoes

prepared crust

◼ Warm the crust in the oven at 300 degrees for 5 minutes. Squeeze the garlic onto the crust and discard the husks. Spread the softened garlic on the bottom of the crust. Layer the cheese next and pipe or spread the whipped potatoes over the cheese. Place the tart under an overhead broiler until it begins to brown.

To serve: Cut the tart into 10 slices while it is still warm. Garnish the top with basil leaves.

Game

Ragout of Beans with Roasted Venison Chop

Yield 8 servings

Venison can be tough to find in many markets. With a bit of research you can often locate a source by having your butcher special order it for you. You might even have luck by having a restaurant with whom you have a rapport order it for you. The most readily available is usually red deer. In Idaho there are a few producers of fallow deer, which is as good if not better.

For the beans:

Combine the pinto, navy, and red beans in a stockpot with ½ gallon of water and allow to soak overnight. Strain the water off the beans and cover with the other ½ gallon of water. Add rosemary and enough sea salt to the water so that it is mildly salty. Cook the beans at a simmer for 45 minutes to an hour or until the beans are tender. Strain the water off the beans and set aside.

In another stockpot heat the oil and add the shallots and peppers. Sauté over medium heat until the shallots become translucent and the peppers soften. Deglaze the pan with the red wine. Then, pouring through a cheesecloth-lined sauce strainer, add the mushroom and venison stocks. Add the beans and cook at a very low simmer for 20 minutes or until the liquid is reduced by two-thirds. Season the ragout with sea salt and black pepper to taste. Slice the morels in ½-inch rings and gently stir into the ragout, being careful not to tear the mushrooms.

1/2 cup dried pinto beans

1/2 cup dried navy beans

1/2 cup dried light red kidney beans

1 gallon cold water

¼ cup extra virgin cold pressed olive oil

3 medium shallots, peeled and diced fine

1 red bell pepper, cored, seeded, and diced fine

1 yellow bell pepper, cored, seeded, and diced fine

1 cup dried morel mushrooms, reconstituted in 1 quart warm water

1 cups mushroom broth, reserved from reconstitution of morels

2 cups venison stock (Use veal if venison is not available.)

½ cup Cabernet Sauvignon

1 sprig fresh rosemary

ground sea salt, to taste

fresh ground black pepper, to taste

For the venison:

1 8-chop rack of venison

sea salt

coarse ground black pepper

3 tablespoons fresh thyme leaves

1-cup canola oil

■ Season the venison racks with the salt, pepper, and thyme leaves. In a large skillet heat the oil and brown the venison completely on all sides. Remove the venison from the pan and place it in an oven-safe pan and into a 350-degree oven. Cook the venison for 15 to 20 minutes or until the meat reaches an internal temperature of 130 degrees. Remove the venison from the oven and allow to rest on a cutting board for 5 minutes prior to cutting it into chops.

To serve: In 8 warmed entrée bowls, ladle 1 cup of the bean ragout (removing the rosemary sprigs) and an additional ¼ cup of the juices from the ragout. Place a venison chop over the ragout and garnish with a fresh sprig of rosemary.

Peppercorn Roasted Elk Loin with Tomato and Rosemary Coulis

Yields: 6 large servings

Backstrap, or tenderloin, is often the tenderest meat. It generally has very low fat content and as a result does not often lend to cooking much past medium-rare. The beauty of this recipe is that the coating of herbs and cracked black peppercorn protects the loin to seal in flavor and juices.

For the coulis:

■ In a saucepan heat the oil and quickly blanch the garlic. Add the tomatoes, stock, and sprigs of fresh rosemary and bring to a simmer. Cook the mixture until the liquid is reduced by half. Remove the rosemary sprigs and place the sauce in a blender to process until smooth. Return the sauce to the pan and season with salt and pepper. Heat prior to serving.

1 16-ounce can stewed tomatoes

3 large sprigs of fresh rosemary plus extra for garnish

12 ounces stock from elk bones (or 1 can beef stock)

1 clove garlic (chopped fine)

2 teaspoons olive oil

salt and fresh ground black pepper to taste

For the elk loin:

■ In a pan, heat the olive oil; season the elk with salt and coat with a generous coating of black peppercorns and Herbes de Provence. Sear the elk on all sides and place in a 350-degree oven to finish cooking to desired doneness. Turn frequently so that the elk loin does not get too overly brown on any one side. Remove the loin from the oven and allow to sit on a cutting board for 3 to 4 minutes prior to service.

1 40- to 48-ounce piece trimmed center cut elk loin

1 tablespoon cracked black peppercorns

2 tablespoons Herbes de Provence

1 teaspoon salt

1 ounce olive oil

To serve: On a warm entrée plate, place 2 ounces of the warm tomato coulis. Carve the elk loin into 36 medallions being careful not to scrape off the peppercorns or herbs. Shingle three medallions over the tomato sauce. Garnish the plate with your favorite potato dish; add vegetables and any extra sprigs of the rosemary.

Beef, Lamb, *and* Pork

Beef Sate with Peanut Sauce

Yield: 6 to 8 servings

You don't have to use tenderloin for this, but it certainly yields a great end product. If you are serving beef for an entrée, buy a little extra and commandeer some for this dish.

For the beef:

2 pounds strip loin or tenderloin, all fat and connective tissue removed

½ cup soy sauce

½ cup sherry

2 cups plus ½ cup peanut oil

2 ounces gingerroot, grated

1 teaspoon sesame oil

1 teaspoon crushed red pepper flakes

1 tablespoon roasted garlic

32 bamboo skewers

■ Cut the beef into 1-ounce cubes and slide onto the pointed end of the bamboo skewers. Combine the soy sauce, sherry, ½ cup of peanut oil, crushed red pepper, grated gingerroot, sesame oil, and garlic in a small bowl and whisk to combine. Marinate for 2 hours in the refrigerator. Heat the 2 cups of peanut oil in a small saucepan to 375 degrees (just before smoking) and submerge the meat side of the skewers into the oil for 60 seconds. The meat should be brown on the outside and still quite rare in the center.

For the peanut sauce:

1 cup blanched unsalted peanuts

¼ cup cilantro leaves

½ cup rice wine vinegar

¼ cup soy sauce

1 teaspoon roasted garlic

2 teaspoons peeled, grated gingerroot

1 teaspoon Siracha (Thai chili paste)

12 cilantro sprigs

■ Roast the peanuts on a sheet pan in a 400-degree oven for 16 to 18 minutes or until they are golden brown. Combine the peanuts with the remaining ingredients in a food processor until smooth. To attain the proper viscosity of the sauce add a little water with the machine running. The sauce should have the consistency of heavy cream, and not peanut butter.

To serve: Place the peanut sauce in a bowl in the center of a platter and arrange the beef around the sauce. Garnish the sauce with chopped roasted peanuts and the platter with cilantro sprigs.

Herb-Roasted Pork Loin

Yield: 6 servings

While not as prevalent as the beef industry in Idaho, the pork industry still flourishes. Thanks to the modern advances in antibiotic technology, it is now both safe and recommended that you eat pork cooked medium to medium-rare.

For the pork loin:

40 ounce trimmed center cut pork loin

2 tablespoons Herbes de Provence

salt

fresh ground black pepper

2 teaspoons chopped fresh garlic

½ julienne red onion

1 tomato, diced

6 ounce white wine

6 ounce pork or chicken stock

1 ounce blended olive oil

■ Heat the olive oil in a pan. Season the pork with salt and coat with a generous coating of Herbes de Provence. Sear the pork on all sides and then pour off any excess olive oil. Add the garlic and onions and cook for 1 minute prior to adding the tomato, wine, and stock. Finish in the oven at 350 degrees until just barely cooked through or to desired doneness.

To serve: Carve the pork loin into medallions, being careful not to scrape off the peppercorns or herbs. Place the tomato and onion mixture on the bottom of a warm entrée plate and shingle six to eight ounces of the pork medallions over it.

Roasted Leg of Lamb with Great Northern Bean Puree

Yield: 8 servings

For pure juiciness and flavor, it is hard to beat a roasted leg of lamb. Have your butcher bone the leg and remove the shank and prepare it for roasting. I don't want to completely discourage you from trying this yourself, however, this is best left to the more experienced. Do, however, get the bone from the butcher, since you need it to prepare the bean puree.

For the lamb:

1 leg of lamb, boned and bound with roast netting

2 tablespoons roasted garlic puree

3 tablespoons extra virgin olive oil

1 tablespoon fresh thyme leaves

1 tablespoon fresh rosemary leaves

kosher salt

fresh ground black pepper

■ Preheat oven to 450 degrees (or its highest setting). In a food processor, combine the garlic, oil, and herbs and process until it becomes a smooth paste. Season the lamb leg on all sides with the salt and pepper. Place the lamb leg on a rack in a roasting pan with the fat cap up and coat the top with a thin layer of the garlic and herb puree. Place the pan in the oven and cook for 15 minutes or until it browns evenly. Reduce the heat to 275 degrees and cook for about 1 hour and 15 minutes or to the desired doneness. I recommend about 130 degrees for medium-rare. Allow the roast to rest for at least 15 minutes prior to carving.

■ Drain the water from the soaked beans and rinse thoroughly. Place the beans in a stockpot with ½ gallon of salted water and bring to a simmer. Cook until tender, about 1 hour. Drain the water off the beans and set aside. In a large sauté pan heat the oil and sauté the onion until translucent. Add the tomatoes and rosemary and cook for an additional 2 minutes then deglaze with the red wine. Transfer the sauté to a food processor or blender and add the vinegar, butter, and lamb stock (reserving 1 cup for presentation) and process until smooth. Season the puree to taste with the salt and pepper and keep warm until service.

To serve: Warm and season the lamb stock to taste. In warm bowls place ¾ cup of the bean puree in the center and ladle an ounce of the lamb stock around it. Remove the roast netting from the lamb leg and slice in ½-inch-thick slices. Serve the lamb over the bean puree and pour the juices from carving over the lamb.

For the bean puree:

1 cup dry northern beans, soaked in cold water overnight

2 large ripe tomatoes, skinned, seeded, and chopped

½ white onion, skinned and diced fine

1 tablespoon blended olive oil

2 teaspoons fresh rosemary leaves

2 cups plus 1 cup rich lamb stock

2 tablespoons red wine vinegar

1 tablespoon roasted garlic puree

kosher salt to taste

fresh ground black pepper, to taste

1 tablespoon butter

Lavender Marinated Lamb Skewers

Yield: approximately 24 skewers

Try to buy fresh spring lamb that has not been frozen. Lamb sirloin or boned leg works well for this, but you must trim all fat and silver skin (connective tissue) from the meat. Then cut the meat into 1-ounce medallions and place the meat on a layer of plastic wrap. Cover the medallions with plastic wrap also and pound the lamb with a meat hammer until it has a uniform depth of about ¼ inch.

For the lamb:

■ Combine ingredients thoroughly. Allow the lamb to marinate for at least 2 hours.

48 1-ounce pieces of tenderized lamb leg, sirloin, or tenderloin medallions

½ cup olive oil

½ cup dry sherry

¼ cup soy sauce

1 tablespoon fresh rosemary sprigs (Dry will do if fresh is unavailable.)

1 teaspoon minced fresh garlic

1 teaspoon fresh ground black pepper

2 tablespoons dried lavender

For the skewers:

24 bamboo or metal skewers

1 large red onion cut into 24 1-inch by 1-inch sections

24 cherry tomatoes

24 button mushrooms rinsed well

48 marinated lamb medallions

■ On each skewer place a cherry tomato then a medallion of lamb then a piece of onion then another medallion of lamb and finally a mushroom. Place the skewers on your barbecue. If you want a rich smoke flavor, throw a handful of alder or applewood chips on the grill just prior to placing the skewers on the grill. Lamb retains its flavor best medium-rare, which is achieved quite quickly, 1 minute or so on each side.

To serve: These skewers are great either hot or cold. Either way just arrange them on a platter with sprigs of fresh herbs for garnish.

Escalope of Pork with English Crumb Crust, Lingonberries, and Wild Mushroom Risotto

Yield: 6 servings

There are several different cuts of pork that work well for this dish. Pork loin as well as pork sirloin work best. You wouldn't want to use tenderloin since it has a tendency to disintegrate during the pounding process.

For the pork:

6 4- to 5-ounce medallions of pork

2 teaspoons kosher salt

1 teaspoon fresh ground black pepper

2 teaspoons fresh thyme leaves

flour for dusting

4 eggs whisked with 1 tablespoon water

3 cups breadcrumbs, fine

2 cups canola oil

1 cup lingonberry preserves

■ Place the pork between two sheets of plastic wrap and pound firmly with a hammer until the pork is a uniform ¼-inch thickness. Be careful not to tear the meat. Peel the plastic away from the pork and season both sides with thyme, salt, and pepper. Dust the escalope with flour and then coat thoroughly with the egg wash. Cover completely with the breadcrumbs but do not pack them on; that takes away from the crispness of the finished product. Heat the oil in a skillet to 375 degrees—just prior to reaching the smoke point. Place the breaded pork in the oil and cook for 45 seconds or until crisp and brown. Turn the pork and repeat the process. Because it is hard to fit more than one piece of pork in the pan at a time, you need to place the cooked pieces in a 250-degree oven on a baking sheet to keep them warm while you finish the other pieces.

■ Combine the sherry or sauterne with the stock in a pan and keep it just off the boil. In a nonstick skillet, heat the oil over medium heat and add the onions. Sauté the onions for 3 minutes or until soft and translucent. Keep the onions moving so they do not brown at all. Add the mushrooms and rice and sauté for 3 more minutes, continuing to stir or toss frequently so that the rice does not brown. The rice may crackle a bit and that's all right. With a 2-ounce ladle add the stock one ladle at a time allowing it to be absorbed prior to adding another ladle. Repeat this process until all the stock has been added. Check the rice to make sure it is cooked through but somewhat still al dente and season with salt and pepper to taste.

To serve: Place a serving of risotto on a warm plate and lay the pork over it. Place a dollop of the lingonberry preserves over the pork and garnish with a quarter lemon for squeezing.

For the risotto:

1 ½ cups aborio rice (Use short grain or pearl rice.)

1 ounce olive oil

1 white onion, diced very fine

3 cups warm pork stock

1-cup sherry or sauterne cooking wine

1-cup julienne wild mushrooms (Use shiitake, crimini, oyster, chanterelle, or morel.)

½ teaspoon fresh ground black pepper

kosher salt, to taste

lemon wedges

Prime Beef Tenderloin
with Wild Mushroom Ragout

Yield: 2 servings

Beef tenderloin can be expensive and, as a result, you'll want to be careful with your purchase. Look for well trimmed meat with the sinewy fat cable removed. Tell your butcher you want "filet mignon" and not just a "chunk of tenderloin."

For the beef:

■ Season the beef with the kosher salt and pepper and place in the smoking oven. Smoke the beef at extremely low temperature for ½ hour. Remove the beef and allow cooling. Once cooled, lightly season the steak with olive oil and cook in a 450-degree oven until cooked to your desired doneness. Prior to service, brush the meat with olive oil to make the beef shiny.

16-ounce beef tenderloin, peeled
kosher salt
fresh ground black pepper

For the ragout:

■ Combine all ingredients except the salt in a nonreactive saucepan and low boil until reduced by half. Season with the salt.

1 cup brown stock
1 cup red wine
½ cup very fine julienne wild mushrooms
8 green peppercorns
1 tablespoon tomato paste
kosher salt, to taste

▓ Boil the potatoes in lightly salted water until soft. Strain the potatoes and blend with a mixer until smooth. Add the butter, sour and heavy cream, and mix until blended. Stir in the corn and basil and season to taste.

To serve: On the left center of a plate, ladle 2 ounces of the mushroom ragout and place the steak on top of it. To the right of the steak, pipe 5 ounces of the mashed potatoes from a piping bag with a large star tip (or mound the potatoes if not using a piping bag). Serve with fresh, seasonal vegetables.

For the potatoes:

2 large russet potatoes, peeled and chopped

1 ear fresh corn

2 leaves fresh basil, fine julienne

2 tablespoons butter

1 tablespoon sour cream

2 tablespoons heavy cream

kosher salt, to taste

fresh ground black pepper, to taste

▇ *Glossary*

Aborio rice: Italian short grain or pearl rice used to make risotto, which literally means "little rice." The best strains are grown in central Italy in the Po Valley, but there are high-quality aborio rices grown around the world.

Bisque: A seasoned shellfish puree or broth used as the basis for soup and then usually "fattened" with heavy cream.

Black peppercorns: A condiment derived from the pepper plant (*piper nigrum*). Black peppercorns are whole red peppercorns that turn black when dried. The best flavor effect is derived from black pepper that is cracked or ground just prior to being used.

Buttermilk: A slightly sour milk product obtained after churning cream. Sometimes used in cheese making but generally used in America for emulsifying bread and pastries.

Canola oil: A light clear cooking oil derived from the flowers of the canola plant. Great oil for sautéing and frying because of its particularly low amount of solids that allow for a very high smoke point.

Caper: The flower bud of a caper bush usually grown in Eastern Asia. The buds are generally pickled in vinegar giving them a piquant flavor that lends itself well to rich fishes and meats.

Caviar: Real caviar is the salted and cured fish eggs from various strains of sturgeon. The best caviars are sold fresh, but lesser grades are often pasteurized. Often caviar is used as a euphemism for any brined fish eggs, such as salmon.

Cayenne: A powder derived from dried, red Mexican chilies. Very hot and best used in minute quantities to give a dish a subtle lift as opposed to being used for "heat" alone.

Chanterelle mushroom: A golden brown, funnel-shaped mushroom with large gills extending down the stalk. They are best if cooked somewhat slowly or introduced to a dish during the simmering process since they can become hardened by flash cooking.

Chevre: A broad term to describe a number of different preparations of goat's milk cheeses. For the purposes of this book it refers to a creamy white and mild goats milk cheese of which Idaho has several outstanding producers.

Chives: A plant related to the spring or green onion that produces a long thin green grasslike stump. The blades are chopped and used as a flavorful garnish that adds a fresh flavor to dishes.

Cilantro: Often referred to as "Chinese parsley," a real staple in Mexican cooking. Cilantro has a very "alive" flavor that is truly distinct. For our purposes it is mostly used in salsas and other fresh and uncooked applications.

Clarified butter: Pure butterfat that has been separated from the whey, salts, and water that whole butter contains. The best butter to use for sautéing because it has much of the flavor of butter without the solids that so readily burn.

Coulis: A liquid puree of cooked and seasoned vegetables, shellfish, or fruits. It can either be used to enhance the flavor of sauces or as the sauce itself.

Crawfish: A crustacean resembling a small lobster. Most of the flesh in a crawfish is located in its tail and is best extracted by first cooking then cracking the shell.

Crimini mushroom: A young Portobelo mushroom with a brown cap and black gills. Mild in flavor and best if the gills are removed before using, since they tend to darken and discolor a dish.

Cumin: A spice widely associated with Mexican cuisine. Cumin powder is the result of crushing the roasted long spindle shape. Used for centuries there are even biblical references of its use in breads.

Dry sherry: The well-known fortified wines of Spain. All sherry starts out dry after a vigorous fermentation that turns all sugars into alcohol. The wine is then fortified with brandy and matured in casks.

Eggplant: An oval- or elliptical-shaped fruit with a purple skin that protects a white, soft flesh. Originating in India, the eggplant was not often used until introduced to Italy in the 15th century.

Filet of citrus: The process of removing the inner flesh of citrus fruit (oranges, lemons, limes, and so forth) by cutting it out of the interior connective tissue. It is most often used as an edible and flavor-enhancing garnish in salads and sauces.

Filo dough: A layered pastry popular in the Mediterranean for dishes like *spanikopeta*. Often the pastry layers are separated and brushed with butter before being reassembled and used as a wrapping.

Fontina cheese: An Italian cow's milk cheese with at least 42 percent butterfat. Young fontina has an elastic texture that melts well and a mildly nutty flavor. Aged fontina has the texture of Parmesan and is used as a garnish over pastas and salads.

Food processor: Electrically powered kitchen equipment that saves time in the preparation of food items for recipes. Some just consist of a bowl with a blade, but more elaborate units can be purchased with cheese grating attachments, meat grinders, and even dough kneaders. One of its greatest assets is the ability to emulsify sauces and dressings.

Fritter: A preparation whereby a piece of raw food is coated in batter and/or breading and deep-fried in lard or oil.

Ginger root: A plant native to Southeast Asia that is cultivated in tropical countries for its spicy root. Can be used fresh or dried and powdered.

Green peppercorns: Unripe peppercorns packed either dry or pickled in vinegar or brine. Less pungent and more fruity than the fully mature berries of the black peppercorn.

Heavy cream: A dairy product that results from the skimming of the top layer of fat off milk. Heavy cream is at least 40 percent butterfat and is a higher grade than whipping cream that is at least 35 percent. The uses of heavy cream are almost limitless; however, it is most often used to "fatten up" soups and sauces.

Herbes de Provence: Herb mixture from the Provence region of France. The mixture consists of thyme, rosemary, bay, lavender, basil, and savory.

Hungarian paprika: The shrub paprika pods originated in America and found their way back to Europe with Christopher Columbus. During the 19th century, Hungarians adopted this spice to flavor dishes like goulash. The best paprika is said to come from Szeged in the south of Hungary and is harvested from "pink" peppers that have bold flavor and no bitter aftertaste.

Jalapeño: A small green chili pepper that is extremely hot and should be used sparingly. These peppers can be made less fiery by removing the seeds and soaking the flesh in ice water before use. An oil called capsaicin accounts for its hot taste.

Jicima: Many call this brown-skinned tuber a Mexican potato. Originally found in the Amazon basin, jicima found its way through Mexico and is common in many of that nation's salsas and salads. Raw, it has a fresh flavor that is a cross between an apple and a turnip.

Kosher salt: Literally, this means salt that is prepared according to Jewish dietary laws. More practically it is a coarse ground noniodized salt.

Lavender: The dried flowers from a lavender plant that grows wild in many parts of Idaho. Many recipes using lavender come from Southern France where it often accompanies lamb.

Leek: Believed to be derived from a strain of garlic from the Near East, leeks consist of a small bulb with a stem of leaves that form a rather solid shaft. Generally only the white of the leek is used with the green tops reserved for stocks or pureed for soups. The layers of a leek tend to trap dirt and must be washed thoroughly before use.

Lemongrass: Predominately used in Thai cuisine it resembles a large scallion. It has an aromatic citrus taste and can be used in either sweet or savory applications.

Macadamia nuts: Originating in Australia where it is referred to as the Queensland nut, macadamia nuts in America are generally grown in Hawaii. With an unmistakable tropical almost coconut-like flavor and a crisp yet soft texture, they lend to both sweet and savory applications.

Marinade: A seasoned liquid in which meat, fish, poultry, or vegetables are steeped for varying lengths of time to enhance their flavor.

Medallion: An item of food cut into round or oval shape. Medallions of varying thicknesses can be prepared from meat, poultry, fish, and shellfish.

Morel: A rare but tasty mushroom that is prolific in the pine forests of Idaho in the spring and very occasionally in the fall. Morels have a conical cap that is furrowed and as a result must be well cleaned to rid it of any dirt or parasites. Generally there are two strains found in Idaho: those with a dark brown or black cap and the larger gray type.

Nutmeg: The seed of a nutmeg tree native to Indonesia. Nutmeg has a spicy flavor and aroma and is always used grated.

Olive oil: For the purposes of this book only cold pressed olive oil is used. This unrefined process does not remove the rich olive flavor since it is derived from simply pressing olives. With this in mind it is not the best choice for cooking since it has too many solids to achieve high temperatures and should be treated as more of a seasoning. Blended olive oil, as referred to in many of the recipes, is one part extra virgin olive oil and two parts canola oil.

Oyster mushroom: An ear-shaped gray or grayish brown mushroom, which grows in clumps on deciduous trees and stumps. Young mushrooms are best with firm and flavorful flesh and can be used in their entirety. As they mature the caps are still fine, but often the stems become too fibrous and must be discarded.

Oyster sauce: Originally from the canton region of China oyster sauce is made from oysters, water, and salt. Inferior brands contain cornstarch and have given the sauce a bad name, but high quality brands can be a delicious addition to a range of dishes.

Poblano chili: A dark green chili that tapers down to a point and is about four to six inches long. This chili is the runaway favorite of rellenos. It's relatively mild on the heat scale and is best when roasted and peeled.

Peanut oil: Peanut oil has a mild taste, but more importantly a very high smoke point. This makes it an ideal oil for attaining a crisp quality in fried foods.

Polenta: A cornmeal porridge that is a traditional, basic meal in northern Italy. The porridge can be cooled and cut into various shapes and grilled, fried, or smoked for an accompaniment.

Potstickers: A fried then steamed dumpling with two distinct textures of Asian descent. They can be filled with meat, seafood, and/or vegetables.

Prosciutto: An Italian word for ham, especially raw (cured) hams that are not smoked.

Puree: A cooked and strained, smooth essence of fruit or vegetable. Fruits and vegetables that are too thin to make a puree can be bound with starch to achieve the desired viscosity.

Ragout: A stew made from meat, poultry, game, fish or vegetables cut into consistent size and shape and cooked in a seasoned liquid.

Relish: A condiment that originated in India. Relish resembles chutney in many ways; however, a relish is often more spicy, piquant, and full flavored.

Rice wine vinegar: A golden-colored vinegar made from distilled rice mash. It can be purchased either plain or seasoned, which has a much sweeter flavor. Rice wine vinegar adds a pleasant acidity to foods.

Russet potato: A large potato that grows prolifically in Idaho. This is the potato many refer to as a "baker." It has a somewhat fibrous skin that protects an abundant amount of white creamy meat.

Sage: A perennial herb that grows in temperate climates. The leaves have an aromatic and sometimes-bitter flavor and a wide variety of uses from meats and stuffings to beverages.

Sate: Any meat that is skewered and marinated then either fried or grilled. Often sate is served with a highly flavorful dipping sauce.

Saucepan: A cylindrical piece of cooking equipment that generally has a handle and a lid.

Sauté: To cook meat, fish, or vegetables in fat until brown using a frying pan. Making a sauce by deglazing the pan with a liquid completes the cooking.

Scallion: A word for sliced green onion.

Sea salt: Salt rendered by dehydrating seawater. The best is the *fleur de sel* that is derived from the top crust that is formed during the evaporation process. Sea salt by nature enhances the flavor of food instead of simply adding salinity, as does processed salt.

Shallot: A vegetable related to the onion that originated in the Middle East. The flavor of the shallot can best be described as more flavorful than an onion and less harsh than garlic. For dishes that call for shallots, there is really no substitute.

Shiitake mushroom: A large-capped, dark brown or black mushroom with a particularly nutty flavor. Remove and discard the stem, since it is too sinewy to be edible. The best shiitakes are about 2 inches in diameter.

Simmer: To heat food slowly and steadily in a sauce or other liquid over low heat, just below a boil, so the surface bubbles occasionally.

Slaw: A synonym for cole slaw. Can be any number of finely cut julienne vegetables marinated in a sweet yet sour dressing.

Soba noodles: Pasta made with buckwheat flour of Japanese origin.

Soy sauce: A basic condiment from Southeast Asia and Japan. Soy sauce is made from soybeans, wheat, water, and salt. Have contempt for cheap soy sauces since they can often be nothing but dark salty water and lack the complexity of the finer brands.

Spaghetti squash: An edible gourd that can be cooked and eaten. When cooked perfectly the fibrous meat can be scooped from the hard shell and resembles noodles.

Steelhead: A large oceangoing trout found in many rivers in Idaho. Mildly endangered because of the damming of rivers and over-fishing. The commercial harvest of steelhead has been illegal for several years.

Stock: A flavored liquid base for making a sauce, stew, or braised dish. There are essentially three true forms of stock: white from poultry, veal, chicken, or fish; brown from beef, veal, or poultry bones that have been browned; and vegetable, which is usually scented with aromatic herbs.

Strudel: Wafer-thin pastry that is wrapped around a sweet or savory filling. The name literally means "whirlwind."

Tarragon: An aromatic perennial plant that originated in central Asia. The green leaves of the tarragon plant have a delicate flavor that is synonymous with the cuisine of Southern France.

Tenderloin: Often referred to as the back strap of a steer, pig, lamb, or game animal, there are two tenderloins located along the spine at the top of the rib cage. After removing the connective tissue the tenderloin is generally the tenderest piece of meat on these animals; however, it lacks the fat content necessary to be truly flavorful and requires a little finesse to become so.

Thai chili paste: Also Siracha, a smooth, spicy puree of red chilies often seasoned with garlic and salt.

Tomatillo: This relative of the tomato family needs to have the husk removed before cooking. The citrus-like flavor lends itself nicely to salsas and makes a great sauce base for rich game meats.

Trout: A fish of mountain streams, rivers, or lakes highly sought after by anglers. Trout are "farmed" in a number of locations throughout Idaho and often fed a mash with high levels of keratin that turns their flesh red like that of a salmon.

Turmeric: A tropical herbaceous plant with an aromatic underground stem. The stem is dried and powdered and used as both a spice and a colorant. Turmeric is a key ingredient in curry powder and the element that gives it the distinct yellow color.

Valencia orange: A strain of orange that originates from the town of Valencia in Spain. The most common use in America is for the making of orange juice. Valencia oranges are harvested in the southeast and southwest throughout the winter months.

Wasabi: A Japanese green powder made from dried horseradish root, sometimes with additional spice powders added.

Water chestnut: The tuber of an aquatic plant originating in southeast Asia having a dimpled and prickly shell that encases crunchy white flesh, with a delicate flavor.

Zest of citrus: The external coating of a citrus plant that is rendered by running a rasp or "zester" along the skin. A fragrant addition to dishes that are enhanced by the floral flavors of citrus that don't benefit from the acidic qualities of the juice.

■ *Index*

Give the Gift of
THE
Idaho
Table
to Your Friends and Colleagues

CHECK YOUR LEADING BOOKSTORE OR ORDER HERE

■ **YES**, I want _____ copies of *The Idaho Table* at $22.95 each, plus $4.95 shipping per book (Idaho residents please add $1.15 sales tax per book). Canadian orders must be accompanied by a postal money order in U.S. funds. Allow 15 days for delivery.

My check or money order for $_____ is enclosed.

Name _____

Organization _____

Address _____

City/State/Zip _____

Phone_____ E-mail _____

Card # _____

Exp. Date_____ Signature _____

Please make your check payable and return to:
Holdthebaby Publishing
1207 E. Lexington Court
Boise, ID 83706